# DELIVER A BETTER SPEECH WITH CONFIDENCE

## Become An Accomplished Speaker Quickly and Easily

### By Charles A. Boyle

© Charles A. Boyle, 1981

LIBERTY PUBLISHING COMPANY
Cockeysville, Maryland

Published by:
**Liberty Publishing Company, Inc.**
50 Scott Adam Road
Cockeysville, Maryland 21030

Library of Congress #81-82439
ISBN 0-89709-026-8

Manufactured USA

**To Karin**

# Table of Contents

# Preface

LIFE HAS BEEN DESCRIBED as the thing that really happens to us as we're making other plans. I had just changed the name of my speech business and was making plans to expand into other cities when writer-publisher Merle Dowd suggested that I write a book about speeches. That seemed like a smart move on his part, since there have only been a couple thousand books written on the subject. But Merle had known me for several years, was familiar with my methods of teaching speakers, and figured my approach to public speaking could help a few people become better speakers without going through the agony of memory courses that don't work* and speech courses that make you work forever.

Most courses on how to be a good speaker require learning memorization and other techniques and call for months of study plus continual practice. Each new speech means starting over almost from scratch. My method, simply put, calls for learning a few techniques for "eye contact" and for conversational reading which

*A student of mine became a firm believer in scripts after taking a memory course from a prominent teacher. A week after taking the three-day course he bumped into the teacher on the street and they carried on a short conversation. The student said the teacher obviously recognized him but just as obviously had forgotten his name.

can make the words from a script come out sounding as extemporaneous as an ad-libbed speech. There's no need to memorize anything and the only practice needed is for those who don't know how to read "out loud" to begin with or one or two "runthroughs" with a new speech before giving it. With few exceptions, speeches, sermons, and opening remarks for seminars and panel discussion should be read and not ad-libbed. Reading scripts effectively is easier and less expensive to learn, safer, and more comfortable for both the speaker and the audience.

Public speaking, however, should mean more than filling a hole in some program chairman's schedule. The opportunity to express your views and opinions before a captive audience is an opportunity lost if you merely fill time. Speeches given to audiences as small as 15 or 20 people can reach out to thousands with your message. As a matter of fact, this book has its roots in a speech I gave to an audience of 25 people at a Rotary luncheon. That talk, "All About Speeches," was published in the prestigious publication *Vital Speeches of the Day*. In that speech I described the benefits of public speaking and why scripts should be used. It prompted Merle to make his offer to me. Only 25 people heard that speech the first time I gave it (I have given it many times since), yet, it resulted in national visibility and set the stage for a book. Like a seed for a tree, giving a speech before one audience, large or small, can and should be, in many cases, only the first step before the harvest. A single speech promoting your cause, your company, or your association can be given again and again to different audiences, printed copies can be distributed, and it may be quoted in the news media and by other speakers. If it doesn't meet at least one of those goals, it probably should not have been given. Thus, to gain the maximum clout from public speaking, you should know more than how to give a speech, you should also know how to get speaking engagements and how to reach greater audiences than those present at the time a speech is given.

In spite of the many elaborate and costly programs designed to teach others how to speak in public, the part-time, nonprofessional speaker needs to learn only a few necessities. Egalitarians aside, some people have an unmistakable talent for public speaking; others simply don't have the innate flair necessary to be a great orator, and all the studying in the world will not convert them to a Winston Churchill or William Jennings Bryan. The nonprofessional *can* learn, however, to get his message across clearly, concisely, effectively—and enjoy the process. This can be done with a couple of hours of reading (not hard studying) and a few hours of practice. Almost anyone can do it, and the proof lies in the classes I have taught to airline pilots, politicians, police officers, and management staffs. For example, Pacific Northwest Bell hired me in 1976 to assist in setting up a Speakers Bureau and to teach their potential speakers. The course is three days long, BUT more than half of that time is used for video taping students' presentations, playing the tapes back, and critiquing. The remaining few hours are used for basic instruction, questions, and answers. Without exception, when the three-day course ends, the improvement of the poor speakers between their first and third day has been phenomenal; the good speakers also improve their ability. All this is accomplished with only a few hours of actual "teaching."

If this book is to be more than a quick, easy course on how you can improve your public speaking, as it should be for a more complete picture on communication, then understanding the news media must be included. Learning about the news media is a natural and important adjunct to learning about speeches since, presumably, we would all like to see our words quoted in the press. Hence, the section on the news media is based on my own experience as a member of that profession dating back to 1952. Again, there is nothing mysterious or difficult about this area of communication. Certain people, corporations, and organizations, no matter what they do, consistently seem to get "bad press" while certain other groups appear to "get good press." Learning how to write a news release or how to hold a news conference won't make that much difference. But the "cold shoulder of the news media" can be moderately warmed up by knowing more about the use of those tools *and* by developing a better understanding of local reporters.

I am positive that by spending a few hours reading this book and only a few more hours on practice, your public speaking ability will improve immediately. You will also know a great deal more about reporters, which should help improve your relationship with the news media.

Unless the subject is absolutely grim, speeches should include light moments and provide audiences with occasional chances to chuckle and a few minutes of enjoyment. It's my hope that this book will bring some enjoyment to those who read it along with useful information to anyone who needs to speak before an audience whether it's 1,500 people at a convention or 15 people at a PTA meeting.

Charles A. Boyle
Bellevue, Washington

# 1

# Speeches Satisfy

Mᴏꜱᴛ ᴏꜰ ᴜꜱ are honored when we receive an invitation to be a speaker at a convention, a banquet, or a service club. But after the first flush of self-esteem begins to fade, each of us reacts to the invitation according to our own measure of confidence, need, aims. Whether or not we accept the invitation depends on a number of personal factors. Some people really enjoy getting up before an audience and giving a speech. Others would rather face a charging hippo than an audience, but, for one reason or another, they must drag themselves away from their favorite television show, go out into a rainy night, drive 30 miles, and give a speech to the annual big bash of the Crocodile Society. Why? Because, they want a bank president to address them and you happen to be the president of the bank that has the Society's $3 million in its vault. Others give speeches because they see a current or long-range benefit to their personal growth, their company, or their cause. In short, people give speeches for the pleasure of it, for the reward, by compulsion, or for a combination of those reasons.

Whatever the motivation, there is no reason why a speech should be an ordeal for the person giving it or

3

for those listening. But there is an important reason, aside from personal inducements, for speeches to be given. In spite of mass communications in the modern world, speeches fill an information chasm. Although we are flooded with broadcasts and publications providing data for everything under the sun and answers to questions we never asked, we get it in bits and pieces. Most of us are informed or misinformed by ingesting fragmented, edited, and opinionated messages, especially from the nation's primary source of news—television. What we need, at least some of the time, is unexpurgated information and the opportunity to question the informant. Speeches provide a vital ingredient for a well-balanced diet of current and historical events.

Shortly before the turn of the century until his death in 1920, Theodore Vail was a colossus in American industry. Newspapers called Vail, the man who built AT&T, the "Cincinnatus of Communications." In his first AT&T *Annual Report to Shareholders,* Vail titled the lead-off section "Public Relations." He was one of the first major business leaders in America to recognize that good public relations provides the proper climate in which to build a successful business. And we all know what a success AT&T is today and has been for the past 70 years. To Vail, "good" public relations meant honest reporting. "If we don't tell the truth about ourselves," he wrote, "somebody else will." Telling the truth about ourselves requires more than a 30-second commercial. Company speakers are an integral part of a total public relations effort. Newspapers, TV, films, magazines, radio, and company publications, all provide one-way communication. But only a company speaker can respond immediately to questions and provide instant feedback to the public.

During the past 15 years, the public's confidence and trust in our institutions—business, government, and labor—have declined drastically. Young people are challenging time-honored values and older people are distrustful of change. In addition to established public relations programs, today's issues call for face-to-face contact with people in the community to answer their questions, recognize their concerns, and express positions.

Speakers are one link in an effort to "tell the truth about ourselves."

Why give speeches at all? Because without them, your message will be incomplete.

From a practical point of view, speeches are essential to meeting the demands and criticisms of today's consumers and constituents.

From an intellectual point of view, speeches have quite often been the launching pads which have moved nations into freedom or chains. Almost every great thought of mankind was first expressed in a speech. Aristotle, Socrates, and Cicero gave speeches which were taken down in shorthand by slaves and then, at least in the case of Cicero, transcribed and sold to the public.

Shakespeare wrote plays—which were mostly speeches.

Walter Lippman pointed out how important it was that America's founding fathers were able to draw on the classical authors and, according to Henry Fairlie, *"First in importance among these were the orators."*

Throughout history the words from speeches have been the banners people have rallied round. In the 20th century, speeches continue as the initial source of many ideas and phrases that move people into action.* Ask yourself, can you remember the words John F. Kennedy wrote in his best-selling (Pulitzer Prize-

*Books may have given birth to Ralph Nader and Rachel Carson, but speeches kept their causes alive.

winning) book, *Profiles in Courage*? But how many of
us can forget what he said in his inauguration speech
—"Ask not what your country can do for you, but what
you can do for your country." This, incidentally, was
first said in a speech by Frederick the First of Prussia
about 300 years ago. Can any of you quote phrases
from the books of Winston Churchill? But who can forget his phrase, "The Iron Curtain" used in a speech a
generation ago at Fulton, Missouri.

From Washington's Farewell to Lincoln's Gettysburg Address, to FDR's ". . . we have nothing to
fear . . .," and Churchill's ". . . blood, sweat, and
tears," the list of memorable speeches is endless.

Good speeches are printed and quoted and remem-
bered.

Why give speeches? Emerson said, "Speech is
power; speech is to persuade, to convert, to compel."
The American statesman Chauncey DePew stated,
"There is no other accomplishment that any man can
have that will so quickly make for him a career and
secure recognition." And, in the 1970's, an executive of
General Motors, commenting on why they have employees at nearly 100 locations available to give
speeches to local organizations, said, "It has long been
our experience that the best way to convey information is on a personal basis."

Why give speeches? Because they satisfy a crucial
need for more complete communication.

## Who Will Listen?

Dr. Edward R. Annis, a former president of the
American Medical Association, began a speech some
years ago by saying: "When you talk about some of
the crowds I have spoken to, it reminds me of a lady
who called me and said, 'Dr. Annis, now that you have
made the big time on television and all that, how
many people do you have to have before you make a

speech?' I said, 'Well, I still insist on two—but I will be one of them.' I will talk to anybody who will listen, because I think it is important."

Before quitting the news business and getting into speeches, it occurred to me that it might help to know if there was a market for my services. Being unable to afford a "market research expert," I took my own survey in about 20 minutes. The formula was easy. Knowing there were 20 Rotary Clubs in the immediate vicinity of my city and that Rotary Clubs meet every week, simple arithmetic added up to about one thousand speeches a year being given at Rotary Clubs alone. Armed with that knowledge, my guess was at least four or five thousand speeches were being given each year in my metropolitan area. I was wrong. There are one or two thousand speeches being given EVERY DAY in my metropolitan area. In metropolitan New York an estimated 10 thousand speeches are being delivered every day.

Service clubs are not the only groups looking for programs, and Lord knows there are enough of them, but there are also PTA's, retiree clubs, Garden Clubs, conventions, school assemblies, and scores of other organizations ranging from monthly labor union luncheons to weekly "establishment" meetings. The audiences for speeches are there—always have been there and always will be there.

The question then is not, who will listen—everybody listens to speeches—but rather, who will listen to *you* give a speech?

The answer is that almost everyone has something interesting to say regardless of their profession. The doctor, lawyer, engineer, company president—all are experts in their field as far as "everybody who is not in their field" is concerned. But even the "nonprofessional" has something of interest to speak about. A used-car salesman undoubtedly has some amusing and fascinating stories to tell about his business as well as sharing some useful, practical advice to all of us who buy a car—100 million Americans. Or, as an avocation he might be a general in the National Guard or a member of the Propeller Club. Maybe he's an expert scuba diver or parachutist. Everybody has a little more knowledge in a particular field than the rest of us. And there's an audience out there waiting to hear about it. But, whether a person is a used-car salesman or the president of the biggest bank in town, an audience expects and deserves more than a mental grasping for words and information from the speaker. If a company executive is invited to speak to 500 people at a convention, he would be a fool to start thinking about what he was going to say to them while en route to the site and then jotting down a few notes while munching on his salad prior to his speech. He would be smart to go to that convention well-prepared. Mark Twain said it takes about three weeks to prepare a *good, impromptu* speech. And yet, the businessman, invited to a small club with an audience numbering 20 or 25 people, might slough off its importance and do to them what he wouldn't do to a large audience—think about what he was going to say on the way out of his office an hour before his speech. Such a lack of preparation too often results in a disgruntled audience, a dissatisfied speaker, and a lost opportunity to present an effective message for your cause or your company.

You have no reason to lose those opportunities—people will listen to you if they are not put under a strain brought on by unpreparedness and fumbling. They will listen if they hear new information; something they haven't heard before: A message.

## What Speeches Do For You, Your Cause, or Your Company

Marshall McLuhan said, "The medium is the message." Meaning, I suppose, that television is where it's all at. A lot of people believe this, and some companies even go so far as to put their entire advertising budget into television. These experiments sometimes fail, and the next year's advertising budget is spread out disproportionately among other media. Suppose, however, that whenever you wanted to reach the public, you would be in a position to command not only television, but every radio, newspaper, wire service, and news magazine to record and report everything you say? Wouldn't that be the supreme communication network? No need to go out and talk to audiences of 50, 100, or 1,000 people. With the flick of a wrist, the entire news media would come to you, and your words would be heard instantaneously by millions of Americans on radio and television and read by millions more in the afternoon or evening newspapers and later in the weekly news magazines. Who would need to make speeches if they had that ultimate communication power? There is, of course, someone who has that power—the President of the United States.

But, in order to summon the combined resources of all the networks to the Oval Room, or wherever they are going to set up the cameras, the President must first have something to say—and he says it in a speech. Furthermore, the President theoretically cannot command any interest in his speech unless it is a "nonpartisan" address of national concern. If he wants to help raise money or support for a congressional candidate in an off-year election, he usually speaks at a $100-a-plate fund-raiser in the ballroom of the biggest hotel in the congressman's city. And, if he wants to raise some dough and drum up support for his own candidacy for re-election, even though he is the President, he'd better be prepared to make hundreds of speeches in hundreds of places. Obviously, the medium is not the whole message. It's only one part.

Back about 1971 I began working for the president

of a large television and radio broadcasting company.
For years, this man sat down every day and recorded
an editorial which was played back the following day
on television and radio. His face was and continues to
be the most recognized face in his city. He could say
almost anything he wanted to say, as long as he could
say it in a minute or so. One day in late 1971 he was
asked to speak to a small convention and he asked me
to write a speech. We sat down together, and while he
told me what he wanted to say in his speech, I took
notes. With the help of research to support his arguments and pleas, I drafted a script and my boss was
ready to make a "live" appearance before the convention. An amazing chain of events resulted from that
invitation. To begin with, he was very happy to receive the applause and cheers of the 100 or so people
who heard him give his speech. He was also happy to
receive some immediate invitations to give his speech
to other organizations to which those attending the
convention at hand belonged. As the months wore on,
he was happy to see his speech published—sometimes
*in toto* in regional or specialized magazines or in part
as the thrust of a story in the local newspapers. He
was particularly happy when his speech won a national Freedom's Foundation Award.

As the months stretched into years, the original
speech kept changing—a paragraph would be taken
out and replaced with updated material. A new
thought would be developed and added in place of an
older thought. The speech grew and lived, and my
boss's "fame" also spread from one city into adjacent
states. Occasionally he gave speeches on other subjects, but mostly he stuck to that one theme about
advocacy journalism. When he first started to give his
speech, he accepted invitations from almost any
group. But, as time went by, he would only speak to
large or prestigious audiences, turning the smaller or
less prestigious audiences over to a vice-president or

the TV anchormen at his station. Once in a while he would ask me to deliver his speech. When I left his employ three years later, he was still giving that same speech, although there was hardly a word left in it from the original script. During all of this time, he had a television and radio station at his command, and he continued to editorialize every day, expressing his opinions on every subject conceivable. In some of his editorials, if the subject were appropriate, he would lift out sentences or paragraphs from his speech and use them to make a point. But he never gave the speech itself on television or radio. Why? For the same reason a president of the United States will give one kind of message to a national television audience and another kind to a gathering of the party faithful. To the television audience encompassing philosophies stretching from the far left to the far right and everything in between, punches have to be pulled, qualifications made, and feelings taken into consideration if there is to be any hope of general receptivity from a mass-media audience. Speeches, however, are aimed at *specific* audiences.

The more closely a message is geared to specific audiences, the more likely it is to be accepted. Without ever saying it, my boss and I knew that his speech— in spite of the standing ovations he received whenever he gave it, in spite of its national award, in spite of its being printed in certain publications—would never be delivered on the air for the consumption of a television and radio audience. We never said so, but we knew empirically that his speech was meant for specific audiences and not for the vast spectrum of thought, prejudices, and intelligences that make up the mass, diversified TV audience. If a speech is to gain the maximum benefit for a speaker, his company, or his cause, it must be geared to specific audiences. This doesn't mean a conservative must only speak to con-

servative audiences, a liberal to liberal audiences, an
environmentalist to conservationists, or a businessman to businessmen. On the contrary, by omitting
inflammatory words and phrases and stressing points
of agreement, a speech is the best way for a labor
leader to reach businessmen or a Republican to reach
Democrats without alienating his base support and
without compromising his principles. I can't say there
is no other way, but a speech is the most effective
way to reach those with different opinions, convince
those with no opinions, and reinforce those who subscribe to your own opinion.

Let's break down the title of this section into
specific examples of how speeches satisfy according
to what they can do for you, your cause, or your company.

*For the individual*—Hundreds or thousands of
people make money by giving speeches. In addition
to the professional speakers who travel the convention
trails, there are the "nonprofessionals" such as political leaders, Watergate repentants, sports personalities, and others who actually make a heck of a lot of
money by getting paid for giving speeches. In some
cases the activities of the political leaders and the
company* with a cause use speeches for a mutual
benefit. For example, a company may want to gain
or cement a relationship with a congressman and one
way of rewarding him is to invite him to speak to a
dinner or meeting with a fat fee for his services. It's
easy to see that giving speeches can be very lucrative
for many people. But, most of us are not political,
sports, Watergate, or show-business personalities in a
position to command large fees for giving a speech.
Nevertheless, the rewards of public speaking can be

*The term "company" in this case can apply just as well to
special interest groups, foundations, labor unions, and organizations.

longer lasting and more beneficial to those who don't speak as mercenaries.

The greatest reward, of course, is personal satisfaction. Aside from financial gain, either as a fee, or as part of your job, public speaking offers you an opportunity to express your views and opinions. If you are not a public figure, or if you don't own a broadcasting company or publication, speeches are about the only way you can reach large numbers of people. Finally, for those of you with a little bit of "ham" in your nature, (and to some degree that's almost everyone!) speeches allow you to perform. When you rise to the platform, the spotlight is on you and all attention is focused your way. There are very few satisfactions that can match a good performance at the podium.

*For the companies and causes*—Speeches can be, and quite often are, the catalysts for immediate or long-range success. Advertising can sell a product and even an idea, such as conservation, if continued over a long period. News coverage, depending on the magnitude and degree of public participation needed, is also necessary for success in promoting causes. Speeches are the vehicles used to get the media coverage necessary to express the company's side of an issue. A specific example of a company using a speech for a cause is the battle between the phone companies and the private carriers. Actually, this controversy involves the entire phone industry and its unions on one side arrayed against private companies getting into specialized phone service on the other side with the FCC and Congress in the middle. There are more than 1,700 phone companies in America, but since the Bell system is by far the largest and in the forefront of the battle, let's use it as the example. The private companies see long-distance telephone service as a money-making enterprise, which it is. They want a piece of the action. By setting up service between low-cost high-volume routes such as Chicago to New York, they can keep their rates low and still make a lot of dough. The Federal Communications Commission thinks this competition to lower rates is a good idea. The phone companies argue that the whole thing is unfair because they have to provide long-distance service between low-volume, high-cost routes such as all the small towns, as well as between the profitable big cities. Furthermore, the Bell System argues that the profits they make on the lucrative long-distance rates help to hold down the cost of home telephone service, which is provided, according to the phone companies, at below cost.

Now, if the whole argument between the regulated phone companies and the private Specialized Common Carriers (SCC), as they are known, would be as simple as the explanation I just used, AT&T, General Telephone, and the other phone companies could saturate television and radio with 30-second commercials explaining the problem and gain the public support they must have to get Congress to overrule the FCC. But, it's not that simple. First of all, most people think phone rates are too high and the Bell System is too big and rich. It's unlikely that public support for the monolithic industry will come from a 30-second TV announcement saying competition from nontelephone companies is unfair. The Bell System must show by comparison and a brief history how it has provided the best telephone service at the lowest cost in the world. This approach requires more time than a brief commercial. It requires a tightly-written speech giving a brief history of the Bell System, how and why it became a regulated monopoly, and how the service and cost to the consumer today compares with other countries. The speech takes 15 or 20 minutes to give and leaves time for questions from the audience. The speakers who give this talk are telephone company employees volunteering their time to tell the story of their industry. Hundreds of these employees are giving this speech throughout the country to thousands of people and urging their audiences to write to their congressmen. Furthermore, newspapers occasionally print excerpts, thereby reaching additional thousands of people. The speakers bureaus for the phone companies also have speeches on other subjects concerning the phone industry and a few speeches that are completely unrelated to the telephone. The purpose of giving these speeches, however, is to perform a public service while at the same time affording the public an opportunity to question representatives of what appears to be a giant, faceless institution. It's easy to get angry with a large company, particularly monopolized utilities; it's a lot harder to get angry with a human being who works for one of those companies when he is making an effort to answer your questions and solve your problems. And that's where speeches come in: face-to-face communications, time to present more information, and the opportunity to receive and answer questions. The outcome of the battle between the phone companies and the private competition is still to be decided as this is being written. But, whichever way Congress rules, the people and the phone companies will all benefit from a better understanding of what makes telephone service in America far better and far less expensive than in any other country in the world.

No other form of mass communication can reach the public with all of the effectiveness of good speeches. There are three unique aspects about speeches:

- Unlike the "remote visibility" of television, a speaker is present, visible, and represents reality.
- A speaker is demonstrable evidence of real concern for the audience and its needs.

- A speech before a live audience is the surest
  way to get a feel for what the public really
  thinks and how it responds to what is said.

## The Message

It's been said that Sir Lawrence Olivier could read
from the telephone directory and an audience would
love it. I don't believe that. I do believe that there are
comedians who could make an audience laugh by
reading from a telephone book while popping their
eyes, waving their arms, and jumping up and down.
But, Sir Lawrence is not a comedian, he is a great
actor. I believe he and other great actors could take a
dull speech and with voice inflections, tone quality,
and other vocal and gesticulating skills, turn that dull
speech into a crowd-pleasing masterful performance.
Unfortunately, most of us are not great actors, and if
our speeches are to be crowd-pleasing, we need to have
something to say. Some people in this world subscribe
to an opposite theory. Dr. Victor Heiser, a missionary
doctor to Samoa, tells about one of the Samoan cus-
toms. More than 30 years ago, Dr. Heiser was being
honored by a native king. Following a presentation
made by the king's spokesman, Dr. Heiser was getting
to his feet to accept it when a native doctor pulled
him back to his seat and said, "We have arranged a
speaker for you." The native then explained that in
Samoa they do not believe that a man who is a good
physician is necessarily a good speaker. "We have our
own speakers who do this on special occasions," he
continued, "and you can be sure that he will say what
you were intending to and do it better."

Evidently, Dr. Heiser must have told that story
many times because American companies picked up
the habit of hiring surrogate speakers during the
1950's and 60's. They would be given a title, usually

vice-president of public relations, and then go out and talk to civic groups about their employer's business. Worse yet, some companies hire speakers who are not even employed at the company and pay them to go out and speak in their behalf. But the public isn't buying the mercenary approach any more. Most audiences would rather hear a less polished speaker who is sincere and knows what he is talking about than a smooth talker who is an outsider telling how great his client's industry is when it's obvious that he's saying it because he's getting paid to say it. Even more damaging is the question and answer period when it becomes obvious that his knowledge about his client's business is extremely superficial.

During the 1970's many companies began to realize that if the message was going to be accepted by the public, companies would have to "speak for themselves." I think they've gone a little too far when bank presidents go on television to do commercials, but in meeting the public face-to-face, not only the presidents but the employees of companies are much better received and are far more believable than the "great" speaker who talks to a group one month about the virtues of the free enterprise system and the next month about the necessity for government intervention in certain industries. Furthermore, the public doesn't like the idea of paying $3 for a product and realizing that 20 cents of the $3 is going toward the salary of a speaker to tell them how low the price is.

For this reason, companies such as Pacific Northwest Bell have a speakers bureau made up of employees who *volunteer* their time to address service clubs, community groups, PTA's, and any other organization in need of a speaker. These employees are given a very brief period of training in public speaking, but the rest of their time is spent doing the job they were hired to do, which may be as engineers, accountants, service representatives, or supervisors. When they are introduced to an audience, they are introduced as a telephone company employee and not as a paid surrogate. Their credibility alone more than makes up for any shortcomings they might have as polished, public speakers.

And, in the next chapter, I hope to show you how to eliminate or minimize those shortcomings. In the meantime, the primary element needed for a good speech, before form and style, is a message. The message must have the following ingredients: knowledge of your subject (the doctor and medicine, the lawyer and the law, the employee and his company), sincerity, and a desire to share your message with others (the employee forced into a speakers program is the wrong person to be speaking).

Which brings up a provocative point. You have a message on a subject about which you are knowledgeable, now how do you share it with others? How does one get speaking engagements?

## How to Get Speaking Engagements

Shortly after my transition from the broadcasting business into the speech writing business a friend remarked that it was too bad that the people who wanted to give speeches didn't have some way of knowing the program chairmen who were looking for speakers and vice versa. We pondered that dilemma for a while and came up with an idea to publish a booklet listing all of the people and companies who had available free speakers. We would then sell the booklet to program chairmen in our area. The plan progressed as far as printing a sample page and cover letters explaining the idea. But, in order to make it work, we needed the names of at least 200 volunteer speakers for the book, and we needed them to each pay

us $25 to be listed. Neither my friend nor I had the
time to go around the city and find 200 people who
would be willing to pay $25 to be listed in our "Speak-
ers Booklet." The project was abandoned. But two
interesting revelations resulted from the idea:

1. Through casual conversations at the end of business luncheons or meetings, we discovered a number
of people who wanted to be listed in the book and
were more than willing to pay the fee. One man, a
travel agent, wanted to buy two listings: one for himself to talk about alcoholism, and another to talk
about travel.

2. One heck of a lot of program chairmen would be
willing to pay two or three times the $5 price we antici-
pated charging for the booklet. It seems that through
word of mouth the idea of our booklet reached the ears
of a few program chairmen who, without ever seeing even a sample page, let alone the finished product,
were quite anxious to get their hands on something
that would gain access to speakers. It's easy to understand why.

Let's look at the average program chairman (PC).
He or she is usually a young businessperson or community leader who belongs to the Kiwanis, Sorop-
timist, Lions Club, Rotary or one of a couple dozen
other organizations. His club nominates him to be the
PC for the coming year, and each week or each month
he must produce a speaker. The first few weeks aren't
too bad because everybody knows a few speakers. But
after our newly elected PC runs through his friends
and acquaintances who are speakers, he has to start
working at his nonpaying, second job. It can take him
three, four or more hours every week to line up speakers—and that's time he cannot afford to spend away
from his paying job. Considering the thousands of
speeches being given every day in large metropolitan
areas and the hundreds of daily speeches in smaller

cities, the demand would seem to be far greater than the supply. Actually, it's more of a distribution problem—the speakers are there. But the part-time program chairpersons don't know where to find 52 good speakers each year, and a lot of good speakers don't know where to find a dozen or so program chairmen willing to risk their reputations on an unknown speaker. The result is frustration for both groups and many of the same local political figures and college professors showing up at luncheon after lunchon. If my booklet had gotten off the ground and spread to every city in the country, a large part of that problem would be solved. Someone with more time, money, and energy than I have might very well put out a speakers booklet for program chairmen. In the meantime, there are scores of ways in which you can let program chairmen know that you are available at no cost as a speaker for the PC's club or organization.

Whatever method you use to line up speaking engagements, make sure *never to ask* to be a speaker—always be in the position of being asked. If you ask a program chairman for the chance to be a speaker, you could both be in an uncomfortable situation. In a sense, it's like inviting yourself to someone's party—it could be embarrassing and it would certainly be bad manners and in poor taste.

On the other hand, there's no harm in asking a mutual friend, an employee, or a business acquaintance to suggest to the PC of his organization that you be invited as a speaker. This is one way to land speaking engagements and probably the most common for the unknown speaker who has something to sell, such as the stockbroker with his talk on the free enterprise system. I'm not knocking it, and for the beginner, it is one of the few ways to get a start.

The best, most acceptable, and longest-lasting approach to be sought out as a speaker, however, is by having a good program to start with, letting PC's know about it indirectly, and then letting your reputation spread. As an unpaid speaker, you'll be in demand.

A good program is simply the ability to give a clear, concise speech full of information about an interesting subject (which can be almost any subject) to an audience which knows little about your topic or has false and incomplete information about it. Most audiences, contrary to the belief that you have to speak in a way about a subject that will catapult them out of their chairs into action or writing letters, merely want to be informed without being asked to sally forth and change the world. I'll talk more about this as well as providing the method for presenting a good speech in the next chapter. First, we have to get the speaking engagements in which to give our good program, and here are some of those ways.

*For Companies*—Print an attractive brochure listing company programs—speeches, slide shows, and films—and make it available free of charge for any organization. Mail these brochures to service clubs, schools, and other organizations such as the Chamber of Commerce. Newspapers almost always mention speakers at garden clubs or at other lesser known groups. They can be good audiences. Many libraries maintain lists of organizations needing talks and provide lists of speakers to program chairpersons. Pick up the list and send out the brochures.

Whenever a company speaker gives a talk, he should always leave behind a handful of brochures listing the other speaking programs his company makes available. Not only will the group just addressed be interested in another program from the same company at a future date, but most people who belong to one club or organization usually belong to one or a dozen others. If they enjoyed the speech, they'll take the brochure to the program chairmen of their other clubs.

Have company-sponsored members (most companies pay service club fees and dues) give the brochure to the program chairmen. In this case, he can be persistent, if necessary. But the member himself, in most cases, should not be the speaker.

Some large companies, General Electric as an example, take out full page ads quoting a provocative sentence or paragraph from a speech given by a top executive. They then make copies of the speech available to anyone who asks for it along with other recent speeches given by the head brass. Advertising not only lets people know that the company has speakers available but also distributes the company's message widely.

*For The Individual*—Any of the above methods which can be done in good taste or without seeming pushy.

Print a one- or two-page biography listing your expertise and/or accomplishments. Have a friend or anyone with a different address and phone number send your bio to organizations you wish to address with a short cover letter. Your friend may say that he thought the group might be interested in you as a program at some future date.

Have business cards printed and available to give to those who ask for them after your speech. I think you'll find that after you have given a few speeches, your reputation will grow and program chairmen will be seeking you, provided, of course, that you have a good speech.

Now that you are convinced that speeches are more than just something to fill up time in the local service club's weekly meeting, that some of the greatest thoughts in history were first expressed in a speech, that there are millions of people out there who are listening to speeches every day, that speeches are a vital tool for getting your message to the public (the best way for *specific* publics), and that you know how to get speaking engagements—the next step is to learn how to give a speech with the least possible effort and the most enjoyment for both you and your audience.

# 2

# Scripts

THE PERSON who wants to give speeches or must give speeches has several primary concerns before worrying about whether or not his words will end up being widely quoted in the news media or by other speakers. Those concerns are:

- HOW to get up before an audience and give a good speech without developing an ulcer.
- HOW to get up before an audience without feeling like an incompetent while talking about a topic he knows like the back of his hand.
- HOW to get up and give a speech and have the audience respond with sincere applause.
- HOW to get up and give a speech and enjoy it so much that he looks forward to his next speaking opportunity.

That's why this chapter is titled "Scripts." Because, with rare exception, every great speech, every good speech, was first put on paper. Cicero, considered to be one of the greatest orators in the history of man, had several of his most famous speeches published as if they had been spoken, and yet they were never delivered personally to an audience.

A few years ago one of my clients was unable to appear at a luncheon at which he was to speak. He sent his assistant to read his speech. She did such a fine job of it that, even though the audience knew she was reading her boss's speech, they gave her a standing ovation.

I'm sure she knew how her boss felt about the issue on which his speech was based. But, she would never have been able to express his exact thoughts, analogies, and arguments which went into the script after careful preparation. In the time allowed for his speech, the boss himself would have been incapable of making the points he wanted to stress had he rambled on the way he did when he was outlining his speech to me. And he's not alone. Try it yourself, sometime. Turn on a tape recorder and give a speech about your field of expertise. Then play the tape back. Unless you are that rare exception, your speech will contain redundancies, pauses, stalling phrases, and probably lack some critical evidence or supportive quotes and information which would have made your arguments more convincing. Now, if you take that tape and transcribe it onto paper, you will find that you have a good start for a speech by simply editing out the redundancies, pauses, stalling phrases, and false starts. More on this later in "Getting it Down on Paper."

One primary reason for using scripts is to avoid making those mistakes in front of an audience. Here's one example of what happens too often when a speaker doesn't have a script. The president of the League of Women Voters came to my club to speak about "Ballot Issues." As the head of a prominent organization, I assumed that she was not a complete novice at public speaking. Judging from her confidence when she began her talk—working from the ballot itself and some notes—it was apparent that she had given many speeches prior to her appearance before our group. About two minutes into her speech, I began taking some notes; here are just a couple of them. Some misstatements corrected by saying, "I said the wrong thing—I meant to say . . . ." A lot of "ah's," long pauses followed by, "I had a leading thought, but I lost it. Oh well." And finally, although this isn't all she did wrong as a speaker, she said, ". . . since 1965-66—was that the year?" She asked the audience which year it was and waited for an answer, but the audience began to argue over it themselves, and while they were kicking that around vocally, she went on with her speech amid mass confusion. Her speech was a disaster. And yet, here was an intelligent woman with an above-average vocabulary and experience in speaking before various groups talking about a subject in which she was well-versed and knowledgeable. On the few occasions when she picked up the voters' pamphlet and read from it, she excelled as a speaker. Unfortunately, those reading occasions were few and far between. How much better her talk would have been had she used a script.

Dr. Harry Emerson Fosdick, the renowned American preacher during the first half of this century, said he never preached a sermon that was not written out fully. In Dr. Fosdick's words, "I do not see how any one can keep his substance serious and his style flexible and varied unless he writes in full."

To put it another way, Edward Morgan, in his *Washington Post* column, described the speakers at the 1976 Democratic National Convention by saying, "You can televise emotions, and sometimes the camera catches a sentence with a thought behind it. *But somehow thoughts seem to arrange themselves in a more orderly and lasting fashion on paper.*" Morgan went on to say, "The advance text of Barbara Jordan's speech looked as dead as smelt. But when . . . [she] got up to the podium to deliver her keynoter, she breathed the fire of burning conviction into her script."

Any leader, businessman, politician, or union official holds strong convictions and has no problem in expressing those convictions when asked a question, giving an order, or during a conversation. But few leaders ever go before the public and try to ad-lib a 15-30 minute speech. Their thoughts and supportive evidence are arranged on paper first—then they read it.

Using a script to give a speech is the best way to arrange your thoughts and to avoid costly or embarrassing mistakes.

But, argue many speech coaches, "It's better to make a few mistakes than to give a stilted speech by reading it." Because of that belief, which has been drummed into us by forensic teachers in high school, college speech professors, and almost every other "expert" from consultants to Toastmasters, we start by trying to memorize our speeches. When that doesn't work, we try to give them from notes and finally, in desperation, from scripts—embarrassed and self-conscious because we've been told by all the "experts" that a good speaker never uses a script.

Let's just take a moment to see why using scripts is supposed to be a poor way to give speeches and see if we can't shoot a big, gaping hole in the arguments. One of the leading speech consultants on the West Coast is quoted in a magazine as saying he teaches his clients to *know* the audience even before deciding what to say and how to say it. A few paragraphs later, in condemning scripts, he cites an example of a speech he gave before an audience of 1,000 Rotarians in Washington State. His speech was on Americanism, but he found out that half of the audience was from

Canada (what happened to knowing your audience?), so he changed the speech on the spot by putting in some stories from Canada. The implication is that if he had planned on using a written script, he would have been unable to do this. Well, this speaker happens to be a real pro when it comes to public speaking, but his advice to the average businessman who has to give speeches is a little scary. If a speaker discovers something about his audience an hour before his speech, so what? What's to stop him from jotting down a few stories about Canadians and adding them to the script if there's time, or ad-libbing them as the pro did if there is no time. At least he would only worry about those couple of memorized ad-libs and not the whole speech. The point is, why sacrifice a good speech in order to be prepared for the unexpected? That would be like a football coach telling his players he'll make up a game plan after seeing what the other team is doing. The most common complaint about the use of scripts, however, is usually a statement that comes from both friends and speech coaches alike. It goes like this, "Say, that was a good speech you gave, but it's too bad you read it. It would have been much better if you hadn't used a script."

Really? How can they know? If the speech was a good one that didn't sound right because it was read, it's because it wasn't read well. It might have turned out to be a rotten speech if it had been ad-libbed. One thing for sure, if it's a good speech, then it's a good speech, and the problem is not *because* a script was used but rather *how* the script was used.

Just one more comment along this line.— This happens to all of us. We all end up at one of those biggies every now and then—a convention or a banquet where some out-of-town pro is the featured speaker. There he is, standing at the podium, enthralling the audience with his humor and glibness. "Boy!" you say to yourself, "If I could only give a speech like that guy." Well, to begin with, he makes his living delivering speeches; he better be good or he won't eat. Secondly, he gives the same speech 50 times a year. Thirdly, listen carefully to what he says, and you'll notice that 90 percent of it is jokes, quotes, and anecdotes. The other 10 percent is a message. Finally, many pros use scripts—it just looks like they are ad-libbing because they've become so good at presentation.

I remember hearing Al Barkan for the first time a couple of years ago. Barkan is the national director for the AFL-CIO's Committee On Political Education—COPE. He was up there at the lectern blasting away at the Republican administration and extolling the virtues of the labor movement. I was fascinated—not by *what* he was saying, but by the way he was saying it. No script—lots of feeling and inflection and fire spewing forth with every word. I was also a bit confused because the rest of the audience, all labor leaders from the local level, were on the verge of complete disinterest. I turned to the gal next to me who had been around the leadership of labor for more years than she would like to admit, and I said, "What's wrong with these people? That guy's a great speaker and nobody's paying attention to him."

She laughed and replied, "Honey, nobody can give a speech like Al Barkan, but we've heard that same speech for years. He must have given it a hundred times."

I guarantee you—use a script a hundred times and nobody will ever know that you're not ad-libbing the whole speech. But, try to give it to a different audience each time.

About the only reason I can think of for not using a script in giving a speech is because there's none available—in other words, the speaker is not prepared.

But I can think of dozens of sound reasons for using scripts. One of the best reasons in the world is to combat stage fright. As mentioned earlier, "There is no other accomplishment that any man can have that will so quickly make for him a career and secure recognition" than public speaking. Yet, for thousands of people, the thought of getting up before an audience to give a speech brings on waves of terror. During the speech, these people suffer from quivering hands and knees and what seems like a mouth full of cotton. They should be enjoying their moment in the spotlight but can't because of nervousness or stage fright.

I know how these people feel because, along with many professional actors and actresses who have suffered from stage fright all their lives, I too have experienced the same symptoms. They're natural and inevitable. But, fear is something else. When Ethel Merman was once asked before the opening of a play if she was nervous, she answered, "I know my lines— what is there to fear?" And that's why, after a brief moment of initial nervousness, I enjoy giving speeches. Because I know my lines—they are right there in front of me. This is true for everyone who uses a script in giving a speech. There are very few people if any, who can get up and face an audience of strangers to give a speech without having one or two butterflies flit through their stomach. But, if they don't have to worry about memory lapses leading to physical collapses, what is there to worry about? Two things: whether the audience will like what you have to say and whether you will say it well. Again, scripts can also solve those two problems. A script can be geared to an audience and, by following it, you will eliminate the chance of a *faux pas* slipping into your delivery. As for saying it well, with a script you can concentrate on *how* you say it, rather than on *what* you say, because what you say has already been decided in the relaxed atmosphere of your home or office instead of under the pressure of an audience hanging onto every word you utter while you are trying to think about what you are supposed to say next. Keep in mind that when Lincoln gave the Gettysburg Address, he used a script which he had written, not once, but five times. He had used parts of the Gettysburg Address in other speeches for years before he spoke those immortal words in Pennsylvania. When he gave that most famous of speeches, he had the script in his hand, in spite of the fact that it was only about two minutes long.

New York speech consultant Roslyn Bremer, the director of Communi-Vu and one of the few pros who feels the same way about scripts as I do, says, "There is nothing better than an intelligently written, well-prepared, properly organized, fully controlled, predictable presentation *read with maximum effectiveness.*"

The real secret of how to *give* a good speech is first to have a good speech to give, and then learning how to *read* a speech with maximum effectiveness.

## How to Use Them

The secret of giving a good speech is to *have* a good speech and then to present it in a manner that will hold the attention of the audience. The logical sequence, then would seem to be, how does one come up with a good speech, followed by, now tell me how to present it!

I'm going to reverse that order because, of the two "terrors" facing potential speakers, the most frightening for the greatest number of people is the speaking engagement itself. Besides, the "big shots" usually have ghost writers responsible for coming up with a good speech, and the "little shots" are handed a script and told, "Give this speech." But if the speech-script itself still worries you, hang in there, and I'll give you a few tips in the next chapter on how to get it down on paper yourself, or how to improve on what your ghost writer has written. But first, let's discover how to present a speech with maximum effectiveness.

The very first thing you have to do is *learn how to read out loud.* Believe me, some of the most prolific readers in the world, people who always seem to have their nose in a book or magazine, can't read coherently when they transmit words from their minds to their lips. By learning to read out loud, I'm not suggesting that you use verbal inflections, facial expressions, or digital gestures. All that's needed is the ability acquired through practice to read out loud—even if it's a monotone* without tripping over every other word.

If you have a problem reading out loud, and many people do because it's done so seldom in this electronic age, then you must train yourself. How? By reading out loud at every opportunity: while driving down the highway, read the road signs out loud; in the privacy of your office, read your mail—out loud. (I'm trying to keep this book absolutely clean, but I would be remiss if I didn't mention that those longer visits to the bathroom can be the best opportunity for reading out loud—there's privacy, daily practice, and quite often broadcast effect). If you can spare the time, set aside 15 minutes each day in any private spot and read the newspaper, a magazine, or anything else that contains a lot of words strung together—but read *out loud.* (Practice with this book, perhaps. You can start right now.) You'll find that within a couple of days that your *out loud* reading, whether you were horrible on the first day or already somewhat accomplished, has improved tremendously. Remember, this is the one

*Actually, reading in a monotone or in sing-song is almost impossible once you learn how to read out loud.

thing that no one can teach you or do for you—only you can do it. It's not hard, but you must practice a few minutes each day until you can pick up any newspaper and read it out loud—cold (without having seen it before)—and only stumble over a few words. You should be able to do this within two weeks, and once that happens, the rest—inflection, eye contact with an audience, and the reading of a specially typed script—will be a snap.

Of course, you want to be able to do more than just read your speech. You want to maintain eye contact with your audience, an authoritative delivery, and respect for what you say and how you say it. Up until now all you are doing is reading words out loud without stepping all over them. The next step is to develop a way to have good eye contact with your audience while you're reading.

Here's where we come to a "gimmick," a "tool" which will improve your out-loud reading ability by 80 percent without the slightest bit of strain on your part. I call it "half-paging a script." If someone were to ask me for one single piece of advice to improve their public speaking (besides practicing out-loud reading), this is what I'd tell them. Keep the words of your speech on the top half of the page and leave the bottom of the paper blank. (Fig. 1). This one effortless act will immediately improve your out-loud reading, your eye contact, *and* your voice. Here's why. If the words on a script fill the entire page, your head dips lower and lower as you read each succeeding line until your chin is practically on your chest at the bottom of the page and the audience only sees the top of your head. Instead of merely moving your eyes up from the script to the audience, as you can do when you're reading from the top of the page, you must "bob" your head up and down as you read the words on the bottom half of the page. The result is a strain on the voice from your

It's been said that if we don't profit from the
mistakes of history, we will repeat them. I don't
think we should repeat the mistakes of the Chinese
Mandarins.

If we're going to have a government of the people,
by the people, and for the people--let's have it--
and not a government of the bureaucrats, by the
bureaucrats, and for the bureaucrats. Thank you.

**Fig. 1A—This is called half-paging a script.**

restricted vocal cords tucked into a bent neck, poor eye
contact from "bobbing" head, and out-loud reading
which is handicapped by eye and voice restrictions.

Try it. Put an 8½ x 11 sheet of paper on a podium
and read. See how much easier it is reading the top
half of the script compared to the bottom half.

Double spacing doesn't seem to bother some
people, but I personally prefer triple spacing.

**Fig. 1B—By keeping the words high on the page with the bottom half of the page blank, the speaker's head doesn't have to dip lower and lower as he reads words on the bottom half of the page.**

Many people who only use cards to give a speech seem to have their heads in their chest all the time.

For good eye contact while reading a script, there's an old saying that goes like this—"Don't memorize, familiarize." I don't recommend giving a speech "cold," but if you are forced into a situation where you don't have a chance to familiarize yourself with the script, you can still have good eye contact by looking up while slowly saying the last two or three words of each sentence. Sentences end with periods, and periods mean pauses. This gives you a chance to

Fig. 2—The higher the words of a script are on the podium, the closer they will be to your eyes without bending your head. Result—better eye contact.

get back to your script with no jerking motions. When you look at the audience on these last words of a sentence, however, don't try to encompass everyone in the room. At the end of the first sentence, look to your right and then back to the script. At the end of the next sentence, look to the middle of the room and back to the script; the third sentence, to your left and back to the script. After all, even if you were giving a speech without a script, you still couldn't have eye contact with everyone simultaneously. See Fig. 2.

Critics will say one of the troubles with scripts is that people keep their eyes glued to them. There's no reason to, but if true in some cases, is it any worse than the person without a script who keeps his eyes glued to the ceiling while trying to remember what he was going to say next?

Anyway, relax. With rare exceptions, there will be very few times, if ever, when you won't have a chance to go over your script thoroughly. By just reading it out loud a few times, half-paging the script, and looking at the audience for the last few words of each sentence, you'll have more and better eye contact than

Most of us have a tendency to read several words
ahead of the words coming out of our mouths. / By
keeping the margins wide, the lines on the page
contain fewer words, and reading them out loud is
easier. / By putting a dark slash mark at the end
of each sentence, / or in the middle of the sentence
if it is a long one, and underlining the last three
words before the slash mark, / we can look up from
the script on those three, underlined words / and
have good eye contact with our audience. / Try it. /

**Fig. 3—Sample script with diacritical markings and wide margins.**

the majority of people who ad lib their speeches.

Unless you are being paid to be dynamic and
entertaining, any audience will appreciate the fact
that you have taken the time to speak to them (assuming the content of the speech is interesting, informative, or both) provided you don't make everyone uncomfortable by groping for words, digressing meaninglessly, and rolling your eyes at the ceiling or your

shoes while searching for a thought or a phrase. The ability to read reasonably well, even with a modicum of eye contact, will assure a comfortable audience. Still you might want to do more than put your audience at ease and impart information. You might also want to spice your words with inflections and emotion. You might want to take a speech which you know is good and breathe some fire into it—well, perhaps not a roaring flame, but a touch of enthusiasm, occasional fervor, a scattering of zest, and moments of calm. With a script this can be done with ease. As mentioned earlier, instead of concentrating on what you are going to say, since the words are already there, you can devote your attention to how you are going to say it. And to have inflection come in the right places, your script can be rehearsed and marked ahead of time.

Some people call this "orchestrating" a script. I have a friend who is a professional speaker (he gives 100 speeches a year at a thousand bucks a crack), and his scripts look like a rainbow. His method of orchestrating is to use a grease pencil drawn through every line and each color has its own meaning—red for slow, green for fast, yellow for pause, blue for loud, brown for soft. Some words and sentences are underlined and others are double-underlined. Another method is to have the lines zigzag on the script by starting in the right-hand margin with the first line and stopping two-thirds of the way across the page, and then starting the next line one-third of the way from the left-hand margin and going to the end of the page. The short lines are great for reading, but the zigzag effect (as well as too many colors) can be confusing. I would recommend, at least at the beginning, using wide margins to keep the lines short, shorter paragraphs for more indentation, and staying away from colors. Instead, use a pencil for underlining certain phrases and words indicating heavier emphasis.

And use the space in the wide margins to write reminders such as "slow," "fast," or "softly."

The more often you use a script in giving speeches, the more accustomed you become to them, and personal shortcuts and habits are developed which make their use easier and easier. Nevertheless, there is one other technique which will enhance your speech delivery immediately without requiring any effort on your part.

Always keep two pages of your script in front of you at all times. For example, when you step to the podium to speak, the first thing you should do is adjust the mike (if there is one) and place your script on the lectern. While taking care of these housekeeping chores before your speech, you might feel like ad-libbing a comment or two about something that has been said by those who preceded you or about something that has happened in the preceding minutes or half hour prior to your speech. At least, unless it's written into your speech, thank the person who introduced you. While doing these things, place the script on the left-hand side of the lectern and then move the first page to the right-hand side. You now have both the first and second pages in front of you. As you finish reading the first page and start to read page 2, *slide,*\* do not turn, page 2 onto the top of page 1. You now have pages 2 and 3 in front of you. By using this procedure, several important benefits occur.

1. You avoid turning pages which, depending on your eye contact, removes the script from the minds of the audience—they never see it.

\*One speech consultant who is a critic of scripts tells about the businessman who "stood up with his big black notebook and then just stood there turning the pages." That could be annoying and certainly would call attention to the script, but by sliding the pages and not having them in a big, black notebook, that particular criticism of scripts is moot.

2. If for example, page 9 sticks to page 10, you have plenty of time to separate them as you are reading page 9 (remember, you are sliding page 9 to the right as soon as you start reading it, which means you have the "whole" page to read before coming to page 10.)

3. Sliding scripts keeps your hands on the podium instead of in your pockets or some other place and improves your posture.

4. There are no unwanted pauses as you come to the end of a page because you merely shift your glance to the top of the next page which is already exposed to your view. And finally, the two pages in front of you at all times adds to animation by forcing your head to move slightly, at the very least.

Following these techniques will make using a script easier to do than it was to read this chapter. Let's briefly summarize:

1. Read out loud whenever possible for the next couple of weeks.

2. Half-page your scripts.

3. Orchestrate your script (but don't overdo it).

4. Double- or triple-space script.

5. Familiarize, don't memorize.

6. Keep two pages of the script in front of you at all times.

Try these techniques the next time you give a speech and your audience will love you, providing that you have a good speech to start off with—one that has something in it *and* that's written for the *ear*, not the eye. Let's see if we can help you get that good speech down on paper or improve what someone else has written for you.

### How to Get It Down on Paper (Yourself or With the Help of a Ghost Writer)

Writing for "the eye" is quite different than writing for "the ear."

Newspapers and books are written for "the eye." Speeches and broadcasts are written for "the ear." Some people, like Winston Churchill, were very good at writing both ways. Others can be very good at one, but not the other. When it comes to writing for "the eye," I, Chuck Boyle, am no threat to people who write books. But, in writing for "the ear," which is how all speeches should be written, I have managed over the years to hold a few jobs in broadcasting, win a couple of honors with speeches, and satisfy a client or two. In short, I don't believe the elaborate techniques ascribed to good speeches by literary analysts, after the speech has been given, mean the analyst necessarily knows what he's talking about. The pros thought Lincoln's speech at Gettysburg was rotten. The people thought it was pretty good.

So, right off the bat, let's set a couple of ground rules for "getting it down on paper." If you want to use an inverted pyramid style, that's fine with me. And, if you don't know what an inverted pyramid style is, don't worry about it—I'm not sure I know either.

Other ground rules are as follows: I'm going to assume that you are acquainted with the English language well enough to tell another English-speaking person what you know about a subject in words they can understand. I'm also going to assume that you are not trying to impress others with how much you know about big words, but rather how much you know about your subject. Finally, I'm going to assume that you are a person who knows a heck of a lot about something and your problem is putting what you know into words on paper which, *when spoken,* will come out sounding natural, clear, intelligent, and, hopefully, inspiring. And you *don't* want to spend five hours a night for the next three weeks coming up with those words.

I can't promise to show you an easy way to write

a speech (it's not easy for me, either). On the other hand, I think I can show you how to come up with a good speech easier than it has been for you (if it has been hard for you in the past). I can help you eliminate a lot of wasted time, energy, and motion getting your speech on paper or help you change that "ghost written" speech into *your* speech.

### Ideas and Words—Keep Them Simple

It's nice to have ideas, but they don't mean very much if they are locked up in your mind and can't be passed along to other people. It's like the proverbial tree in the forest. It falls, but nobody hears it and nobody knows. A good idea is usually a simple idea, that's one of the things that makes it good. But, when we try to explain it to someone else, we quite often embellish it unmercifully or wander afield, making it more complicated and thereby making it less of a good idea in the minds of the people hearing it.

One of the first things that happens to us when we sit down to write a speech is that we run into a mental block because we have been told or believe that a speech is supposed to do certain things. It should have a "beginning" which is supposed to "set the theme" or the "direction should be outlined." Then there is the "main body of the speech broken down into various subsections." Finally, there is the "conclusion" and/or "summary." And if it's going to be a good speech, we are told, it should "motivate" the audience to do something—write letters, march on city hall, or tear down the power company building. Let's get rid of those ideas first.

Fully 99 percent of the people who sit and listen to speeches don't want to be forced into taking on extra work. And if the thrust of your speech is aimed at getting them to charge out into the street or write a letter to their congressman, your thrust will likely be a bust. Most audiences are made up of people who happen to belong to the organization to which you have been invited to speak—Rotary, Kiwanis, political club, PTA or whatever. Half of those people would prefer, if given a choice, to be playing golf or sailing their boat. But, they are there listening to you and they don't want to be harangued, lectured, criticised, or told to storm the bastille. What they want is to be informed. If they can be informed by a speaker who knows what he wants to say (by having it on a script prepared ahead of time), then the audience is going to enjoy it more; and some of those, who earlier would have rather been playing golf, might not be too sad about getting on the course later. If members of the audience leave the room following the speech and can say to their neighbors as they walk out, "I *didn't know* that," in reference to what the speaker had to say, they might even be glad they came instead of going sailing.

The successful speaker is the one who tells his audience about something interesting that they didn't know before ("I didn't know that"), not the speaker who makes everybody squirm or feel guilty if they don't write a letter to the governor.

The preceding might might take the wind out of any ego trip we have about giving speeches and may even prompt us to ask ourselves, "why bother?" It certainly doesn't sound like it has much to do with writing a script—"getting it down on paper."

Well, your "ego trip" as a speaker will be a much more pleasant journey if the audience is with you rather than fighting you. And people *are* going to fight if they are asked to do something they don't want to do. As for even bothering to give a speech if people aren't going to "charge out" afterward, keep in mind that editorials in successful newspapers don't ask people to do anything, they inform and try to sway people to their way of thinking by presenting information from their point of view. Speeches are like editorials—strip mining from *your* point of view—not the ecologist's or vice versa.

Understanding how the audience feels makes it easier to get your speech onto paper, and if you are not trying to come up with a "magic" opening and closing on a rough draft, the speech will be easier to write. And if you forget about charts and roadmaps and outlines, you'll save a lot of paper and a few more headaches.

But rough drafts are a must for quick, easier speech writing.

There are two ways of doing a rough draft. Because I have written news all my life, it's simpler for me to think and type at the same time. For the person who is used to dictating, it would probably be more comfortable to use a tape recorder. Either way, the important thing is to get down on paper (or tape) the main idea of your speech. Don't worry about sloppiness, context, spelling, grammar, quotes, or anything other than the fact that you are a banker, doctor, lawyer, candlestick maker, and you want to talk about your bank and the banking business—or whatever. If you were to tell everything you know, your speech could go for days on end. So, you'll zero in on a specific area of the banking business. Interest rates? How banks make money on checking accounts? Whatever you decide to talk about, pile up all those bits of facts and information you have alongside of you and start writing (or taping) and get it off your chest. Don't worry about the opening—your first facts might turn out to be a good ending. The only thing you want to do is get your ideas on paper—triple spaced. (If you tape it, transcribe it to paper triple spaced). After you have everything you want to talk about on paper—which shouldn't take you more than a half hour or so of dictating plus whatever time it takes to have it transcribed onto paper, or two or three hours of typing if that's the way you want to go—you might look at it in horror! On the other hand, you might think it's not too bad as it is. Have faith. The next step is to take that mess of misspelled words, lousy grammar, redundancy, forgotten facts, and broken continuity, and look it over carefully, inserting the forgotten facts and eliminating the redundancy as you go along.

Look a second time; think about it. Does each paragraph make sense? If it doesn't, you have plenty of space between the lines to change a word or a phrase so that it will make sense. Does it flow? If it doesn't, perhaps page three should be page two. Reverse the pages. Bankers know what the "middle market" means, but will your audience? Add a phrase explaining it. Are there other words that have a specific meaning for your industry, but another meaning to most people? Change them. How 'bout a good favorable quote on money? Most quotes are unfavorable, but in your trusty little quotation book you come across one by W. Somerset Maugham saying, "Money is like a sixth sense, and you can't make use of the other five without it." Throw that into the speech— at the beginning or end—where you talk about the importance of banking.  "Banking is about money. Sight, hearing, taste, touch, and smell are the five senses, but as W. Somerset Maugham so bluntly put it, etc."

You now have a rough draft of a speech saying what you want to say in words you would normally use in talking with your 14-year-old son or daughter.

If your first draft is *really* rough, that is, difficult to read to yourself because of pencil marks, arrows, sentences shifted around, and so forth, retype, or have retyped, the messier pages.

With this reasonably "clean," triple-spaced copy of a rough draft, the next step is to read it *out loud*. That great alliterative sentence may not roll off your tongue as easily as it rolled out of your mind. Or, just because everyone else is starting to preface their thoughts by saying, "Indeed," it may sound phony when you use it. It only sounds silly to say "finalize an upward corrective adjustment in product lines" when what you are talking about is raising the price. But, this reading must be done *out loud*; those tripping words and phrases might be a cinch to read silently, but ambushes orally.

According to identical word tests given to a large sampling of people in 1952 and 1973, it was discovered that the average American's vocabulary was considerably larger in 1952 than it was 20 years later. Although we keep hearing that today's young people are brainier than their parents, don't take any chances—keep it simple, even for young audiences.

What about grammar? Without it, our words wouldn't make sense. Grammar is like a traffic cop at a busy intersection—*but*, as my old United Press stylebook puts it, "Normal conversation, even among professors of English, differs from the written word . . . and rules of grammar are bent, if not ignored . . . . Many rules of grammar may hamper a good speaking account rather than help it." As long as I'm quoting UPI, here's an example of imperfect grammar, but good "ear" writing.

"TENS OF THOUSANDS OF MOSCOW CITIZENS TRUDGED PAST THE CHINESE EMBASSY IN MOSCOW TODAY. THEY SHOUTED SHAME . . . MAO TSE TUNG IS A TRAITOR . . . AND OTHER SLOGANS AS THEY SHOOK THEIR FISTS AND SMASHED WINDOWS WITH STONES.

"THE SOVIETS ANNOUNCED THEY HAD SENT A HARSH NOTE TO PEKING DEMANDING

THE CHINESE END THEIR HOSTILE ACTIONS AGAINST THE SOVIET EMBASSY THERE AND ALONG THE SINO-SOVIET BORDER.

"THEN THEY SENT TENS OF THOUSANDS OF MOSCOW CITIZENS TO MARCH PAST THE CHINESE EMBASSY . . . BREAKING MOST OF ITS WINDOWS . . . AND SMEARING IT WITH RED, BLUE, AND LAVENDER INK.

"FINALLY . . . THEY CALLED A FULL SCALE NEWS CONFERENCE AND ACCUSED CHINESE SOLDIERS OF BAYONETING AND MUTILATING THE WOUNDED IN LAST SUNDAY'S CLASH ON DAMANSKY ISLAND.

"AS FAR AS THE SOVIETS ARE CON-CERNED, THE COLD WAR WITH PEKING IS GROWING HOT."

From a writing-for-the-eye standpoint, the above could be criticized on several points, including bending the rules of grammar. But it "listens good." It's active, it has pace, it's clear rather than confusing, and it builds interest.

My point is that the written word is a subtle and beautiful thing, but writing the spoken word, so that it will be listened to and understood, is an art that depends on simplicity. If it takes something slightly less than absolutely perfect grammar to accomplish this, don't worry about it. You can always polish the grammar for the copies of your speech to be printed and distributed.

The art of simplicity in writing to be heard also applies to other areas—and especially to the words used in your speech.

One day early in 1977 I received my copies of *Vital Speeches* and, as is my habit, began reading all the speeches in it. I came to one called "Technolitics" by a consultant with a first name that was only an initial and some numbers after his last name. The first two paragraphs of this speech contained these words, among others: econometric, progenitors, academe recondite, intuit. The last sentence of the third paragraph ended this way: "and validity is imputed to the last postulate as being autocogent to the exercise." At first I thought it was a joke—like one of those comedians who talk double talk—and that in the fourth and fifth paragraph he would let us all in on the punch line. But, as it turned out, it wasn't supposed to be a funny opening; there was no punch line—the whole speech went on like that. Please—even if you are a college professor speaking to college professors, don't give speeches like that. Don't even write for the *eye* like that, let alone the ear. That's why we have government bureaucracies such as OSHA taking 130 words to define exit as compared to the 23 words in Webster's unabridged dictionary.

My teenage daughter recently started a collection of "gobbledegook" by saving everything in the newspapers referring to it—editorials, columns, feature stories, and so forth. Within a month she had a pile of "gobbledegook" articles high enough to sit on. No need to give any more examples, you can have your own collection of thousands in a few weeks.

In writing for the ear *or* the eye, keep it simple. Don't try to impress anyone and don't use 50 words where five will do the trick. Remember, you know a lot about your subject, so you don't have to puff it up with unnecessary words.

When we speak to people—friend, stranger, employer or employee—we use contractions. We say, "that's", not "that is", "I'm", not "I am." In writing a speech, use contractions. When you read it aloud, the contractions will probably sound a lot more natural in nine cases out of ten. Once in a while, however, to emphasize a point, you may not want to contract words. Then don't.

You have now dictated or typed your speech roughly. Transferred it (or cleaned it up slightly) onto paper, triple-spaced. You have taken out the redundancy and added some points and information, along with an appropriate quote or two, which you had omitted in getting it down in a hurry. The big words, jargon, and tongue twisters have been taken out. You have a first draft that's not too bad. Now all you need is a decent opening and closing and the right length since you've been told you'd have 20 minutes to give your speech and 10 minutes for questions and answers. You could wait 'til you've finished the whole speech, look at your watch, read it, and then see how long it took. But when you're working on a script, it helps to know if you are in the ball park as far as the time element is concerned. Normal out-loud reading speed is 130-140 words a minute. At roughly 250 words to the page, triple-spaced, you'll be in the time ball park with 11 or 12 pages of script. A couple of paragraphs will handle the opening and closing for the speech, with only a minimum effect on the timing. The big problem remaining is, what's the best way to get into this speech and the best way to get out of it?

Take a look at the beginning and end of your speech. Are they really that bad? Perhaps all you'll need to do is change a word or two—a sentence, or a supportive quote. There's no way of telling, of course, without the whole speech in front of you, but generally there are a few techniques that can be used at the beginning of a speech time after time. One is to start out with a question such as, "Have you ever wondered why . . .?" Just make sure the question applies to your speech. Another is to use quotes or anecdotes. Again, make sure they are appropriate to your message, and, believe me, there is nothing in the world that any of us can talk about that someone of stature hasn't already talked about—with quotes! With rare exceptions, every speech should start out humorously. Unfortunately, too many speakers take this to mean jokes which they tell whether the jokes have anything to do with the occasion or not—and worse, whether they can tell jokes effectively or not.

We'll take a close look at humor in speeches in the section "Clients Question Me."

There are those who say the opening of a speech is critical—"If you don't capture the audience with your first paragraph or two, you'll lose them." Hogwash! The beginning of a speech is no more important than the middle or end of it. The fact is, the entire speech is important. Everything you say in it must have some meaning—not profound or earthshaking—simply information about your subject. Some of the information should be unknown to most of those in the audience. Other information should be accepted knowledge or beliefs by most of the audience. Each person is then thinking to himself, "This speaker is pretty sharp because he thinks or knows about the same things I believe." Humor is important in your first words only because it relaxes the audience, which in turn relaxes you. It starts things off on a friendly note. As for the ending, the best ending there is can be used—and should be used—with any speech: a simple "Thank you." I find it incredible that some speech coaches advocate ending a speech without saying "Thank you" to the audience. That's just plain bad manners to have the attention of all or a large part of an audience for 20 or 30 minutes and then to sit down without thanking them.

You might, however, want to precede that "thank you" by quoting a famous person who supports the theories or information which you have just finished speaking about. You may even want to emphasize your main thrust by repeating it briefly and in different words than you used earlier—but don't summarize. If the audience didn't listen the first time you said it, they aren't going to listen at the end. And if they didn't understand it the first time you said it, you shouldn't have said it that way to begin with.

"Getting it down on paper" then, in my opinion, should not be an exercise in diagramming and outlines. The beginning of the speech should be what you have to say to the audience, the middle should be what you have to say, and the end should be what you have to say. A humorous line or two can be added to the beginning and throughout your speech if appropriate and relevant. Quotes can be added to the beginning, middle, and end if they are supportive, humorous, or needed to break up a monologue. Always end the speech with "Thank you."

When your final draft of the speech is completed, have two clean copies typed. One copy is what I call the "working" copy. It is the one that is triple spaced and only goes halfway down the page. The pages should be numbered at the *top of the left hand corner*. This will immediately allow you to see the page coming up as you slide the pages of the script on the podium. Triple spacing will make it easier to read, *and* if in a final rehearsal you find a word or sentence is giving you trouble in out-loud reading, you have plenty of room between the lines to replace the troublesome words. By using half a page and triple spacing, you will end up with a working copy 25 or 30 pages long. Don't worry about it. The other copy to be cleanly typed should be single spaced and go from the top to bottom of the pages. You'll end up with 5 or 6 pages. It'll be a lot cheaper to Xerox for people who want copies. Put your name and address on all copies.

### Ghost Writers

One antiscript argument holds that some people think it's an insult to an audience to read a speech. I think it's a compliment. By putting your thoughts down in the form of a script, you are, in effect, saying that you care enough for your audience's time to spend hours—not talking and rambling—but researching and writing in an effort to give them the best of your knowledge without wasting their time. As for the person who hires a professional to put his knowledge into a concise presentation, if the audience should guess or know that someone else wrote the speech, the person who hired the writer is telling the audience that he cares enough about them to spend his money in an effort to give them the best talk he can.

The problem with so many ghost-written speeches, however, is that they don't sound like the person who is giving the speech.

There are many speeches, of course, that are meant to be interchangeable, and the audience knows this and accepts it. For instance, a large corporation may have a slide presentation or a speech requiring a demonstration of new developments in the industry. Several middle-management or even non-management people might take that speech, and give it to hundreds of different audiences. This is an acceptable practice, and the person giving that kind of speech should merely look it over and change uncomfortable words and sentences. In most cases these are technical talks which fall into the category of "programs" rather than speeches.

Ghost writers, however, are normally thought of as people who write books, articles, and speeches for specific persons who put their names on the material as though they themselves wrote it.

Earl Whitehill, who pitched for the Washington Senators, was given a ghost writer to do a series of articles for the 1933 World Series. The literate Whitehill complained that the ghost writer was making him sound like an illiterate.

Samuel Goldwyn had a ghost writer doing a series of articles for him, but the spook became ill and another ghost was brought in. Goldwyn read the article done by the sub and lamented, "This isn't up to my usual standards."

And then there's the old story about the speech writer who got mad at his boss who had a habit of never looking over the speeches, but instead read them for the first time as he got up before an audience. The ghost writer was really unhappy about the money he was being paid, and one day he handed his boss a sheaf of papers right before a speech. The first page was beautifully written, but when the boss turned to the second page, it was blank except for one sentence: "You're on your own, you SOB."

**MY GHOST WRITER COULD LICK YOURS ANYTIME.**

Presidents of the United States have speech writers—whole teams of them. And some company presidents employ assistants for the sole purpose of writing their speeches.

If the volume of speeches given by the top three or four men in a company is heavy, hiring a speech writer makes good economic sense. Consider the hours that company presidents and vice presidents could spend grinding out their own speeches and how much they're being paid on an hourly basis compared to how much a good speech writer is paid.

For the company president who only gives a few speeches each year, a ghost writer put on a small retainer and paid by the hour per job, also makes good economic sense. For example, let's assume the company president is paid a salary that comes to $50 an hour when vacations, retirement, sick leave, and other fringe benefits are included. If he has to take 20 to 30 hours to write a speech at home during evenings or on weekends, it puts an unnecessary strain on him and affects the job he's being paid to do. If he writes his speech during office hours, the company is still paying for the speech and paying for more time than it should take to have it written—as much as $1,500 of the President's time to get it down on paper.

On the other hand, a ghost writer could write that same speech in ten hours of writing time and another five hours of meeting and research time. At $50 an hour, the speech would cost $750. More important than the saving of $750 is the final product. A good ghost writer, since writing is his field of expertise, should be able to churn out a better speech than the one the company president was about to write.

In using the services of a ghost writer, however, be wary of two pitfalls. The first trap to avoid is falling in with the wrong writer. Make sure you hire someone with a proven record of writing good *speeches* for *other* people to give. The second and most important trap is inattention. The trouble with too many people who have someone else write their speeches is that as soon as they assign the writing job, they forget about the writer. The end result is that the executive takes the finished product and reads it, but it sounds contrived.

If you plan on using a ghost writer, there are two courses you can follow which will lead to a speech that sounds like you wrote it—and did an excellent job of writing it.

The first course is the ideal situation. Here you work with the speech writer by spending one hour with him telling what you want to say and in your own words. He, in turn, should be taping, taking notes,

THE WIZARD OF ID by permission of Johnny Hart and Field Enterprises, Inc.

and asking questions. He should then take the tape and the notes and research material that you have to back up what you say and write a first draft of the speech, adding his own research material to strengthen it. On the second visit the two of you should go over the speech, making sure everything important to be said is said and that it flows easily. Additional material and points can be inserted and the second or final draft can then be completed. The help you provide to your ghost writer is critical in developing a good speech for *you* to give. By taping your words, he picks up your rhythm of speech, mannerisms, normal words you use to describe certain events pertinent to the speech, and your thoughts on the subject. As a writer writing my own speech on the subject of air pollution in Pittsburgh, I might say, "Thirty years ago, a white collar worker needed two shirts to get through the day without looking like he had been down in a coal mine. Today, you can wear the same shirt for two days and it'll still look clean." But my client, in telling me how he feels about pollution in Pittsburgh, might say, "The air has improved here in Pittsburgh over the past 30 years; we are making remarkable strides in the right direction, but we still have a long way to go."

If I were his ghost writer and simply received an assignment to write a speech about air pollution in Pittsburgh and told to be optimistic, I would probably write it as demonstrated in the sample—my style, somewhat flippant, indicating the air cleanup job is done. Which is not the way the client felt at all. But, if we sat and talked about the speech ahead of time, he might very well have expressed the exact thought used in the second example and those would be the exact words I would use in writing his speech.

The speaker and the speech writer working together are the ideal ghost writing team.

The other course that can be followed is to give the ghost writer the subject, your feelings about the subject, supportive information, and some old speeches you have done. This can all be dropped in the mail. Old speeches are critical! Send only the ones that you liked and that sounded like you. The ghost writer can then pick up your style from those speeches.

In my opinion, Franklin Delano Roosevelt and John F. Kennedy were the best speakers among our Presidents in this century. They both worked very closely with their speech writers. Although their writers were excellent, that didn't stop the Presidents from making the speeches even better. One example: One of FDR's writers ended a speech by saying, "We are trying to construct a more inclusive society." Roosevelt rewrote the last line to read, "We are going to make a country in which no one is left out."

Like everything else, the value of ghost writing has its detractors. Walter Lippmann, the patron saint of journalists, said, "No man can write an authentic speech for another man; it is as impossible as writing his love letters for him or saying his prayers for him." Well, Christians might take exception to the prayer part; they've been praying for their friends and relatives and the poor of Russia, India, and China for centuries. As for ghost writing another man's love letters, Cyrano de Bergerac was a real, 17th-century Frenchman. And in the 19th-century play by Edmond Rostand, Cyrano had extraordinary success in writing his friend Christian's love letters to the lovely Roxane. Alas, poor ghost writer Cyrano didn't get any credit for his masterpieces until he was on the verge of giving up the ghost. In any event, Cyrano did write Christian's love letters as well as his speeches, and with a magnificent flair to the benefit of the young musketeer.

Hiring a speech ghost writer, either a "freelancer" or full-time with some other duties (like writing your love letters), depends on your circumstances. Figure out the cost of doing your own speeches, not only in time and money, but in aggravation, and then act accordingly. But if you do use a ghost, make sure you put a little bit of yourself in the speech. First of all, no writer is infallible, and secondly, only you can add the personal touch that will make it *your* speech.

Whether you use a ghost writer or do it yourself, one thing is certain—by having a script, you know ahead of time that your speech is good and that you are prepared. That's 90 percent of the battle.

## Visuals

Is there any way to know which came first—the visual communication or the audible communication? My guess is the audible message. It may have been a horrifying grunt to express displeasure or a purring kind of sound to indicate joy. Then, presumably, came pictures scratched into the sand or on a cave wall to tell a story for which words had probably not yet been coined. Skipping over the centuries like a movie film that lost its loop, we come to the Twentieth Century where words, written and spoken, mingle freely with pictures, still and animated. A flood of communication has covered the earth in greater depth than the Biblical waters of Noah's age. Ibsen said, "A thousand words will not leave so deep an impression as one deed." Along came the *New York News* and somebody else said, "One picture is worth a thousand words." If that were true, we could give a 20-minute speech by showing three pictures. I'm not sure many audiences would appreciate that kind of shortcut, however. Actually, words can quite often draw better pictures than pictures themselves—even animated ones. How often have you read a book and later saw the same story in a movie which disappointed you for falling far short of the joy you received from the words in the book?

Words are images. They seldom need pictures. In fact, words can describe size, big or small, cold, heat, love and hate, more vividly than a photo, a movie, or a video tape recording.

Perhaps it's because of ego, but I don't like to use slides or charts when I give a speech. Subconsciously, I might be resisting the idea that an audience is diverting its attention from me to images on a screen. I believe that anything that needs to be said can be said in words without the help of slides. Besides slides are mechanical things and can get screwed up. They are also a problem in many other ways; they have to be made and transported to the scene of the speech. Heavy equipment has to be lugged around, set up, torn down, and hauled off after the speech is over.

Having said all that, there are times when slides or charts can be very effective props in giving a speech.* For example, a friend of mine was giving a speech on water conservation. He whipped out a large chart and held it up to the audience. While he told them how much water had to go over the dam, the chart showed water cascading through its spillways, some glasses, and some numbers. If memory serves, it required 762 glasses of water over the dam to create one glass of ice water—so much water to produce the electricity to make the ice, so much water to wash the glass into which the ice water was poured so that someone could drink it, and so on. I think he could have made his point without the chart but the chart was pretty—and it was in color. Anyway, he thought

*Sometimes "visuals" or a demonstration is essential. For example, try teaching your son to knot a tie with words only.

it was a great idea for his speech and he was happy. It didn't hurt anything, the audience was satisfied, and that's what counts.

Later on, in the news media section, I mention the visuals that are demanded by TV assignment editors. A picture of a window washer working near the top of an 80-story building will command more minutes in the 6 o'clock evening news than three peopled killed in a car accident. (Unless they have some really good shots of the car accident actually happening.)

Visuals can be very interesting on TV or in a speech. They can also add clarity without strain to a speech. I don't think top executives should use them (former President Ford tried using charts in a television speech one time and it was a disaster), but for most other speakers, good slides, coupled with a good speech, can be dynamite.

A couple of years ago, *Executive Digest* published a list of tips on how to prepare slides (charts) for a speech, and after studying it closely, I can't see where I could improve on it. So, here it is:

> The slides you show to enhance a speech don't have to be elaborate. It's more important to concentrate on clarity, quality, and content when planning and preparing your slides. Here are some tips to keep in mind:
>
> 1. Express only one thought or idea in each slide. Since the visual is on the screen for only a brief period, it must be simple and to the point.
>
> 2. Be sure each slide supports your verbal material. Your aim is to emphasize or clarify by allowing the eye to assist the ear.
>
> 3. Make sure each slide is technically competent. When your audience is concentrating on voice and picture, the smallest imperfections may be noticed.
>
> 4. Keep illustrations simple. Too much detail can be distracting. Keep drawings simple, use lots of white space and readable typography.

5. Avoid too much type on any one slide. A simple graph or line drawing is also preferable to a long list of figures or words.

6. Don't be afraid to use captions.

7. Always number your slides and key them to your script. Make sure the numbers can be easily located by your projectionist.

The physical make-up of a script for a speech using slides also uses half of a page. Instead of the bottom of the page being blank, the left-hand side of the paper is devoid of your speaking words. The left side of the page is used for indicating which slide is supposed to be punched up and any other notes of instruction or reminders. (See Fig. 4)

Presenting a slide-speech doesn't require as much eye contact with the audience, but this doesn't mean no eye contact at all. Visual speeches are very busy. The audience is looking both at the speaker and at the slides. The speaker is working the slides, reading his script, glancing at the slides to make sure it's the one that's supposed to be on the screen, and, while doing all this, trying to pay some attention to the audience.

Unless you have absolutely no choice, try to have your screen placed parallel to the left or right of your podium somewhere between 5 to 15 feet away and angled very slightly toward you. If you are going to use slides at all, try to use a lot of them and bunch them. Work them into your script so that they come into the speech and stay with you 'til you're through with them. In other words, don't have some slides at the beginning, a lot of talk without slides, more slides in the middle, more talk without slides, and then slides at the end. Better to have no slides at the beginning of the speech, slides in the middle, and no slides at the end. By doing it this way, the audience will be much more comfortable—and so will you. When you are using no slides at the beginning of the speech, use the

| | |
|---|---|
| #57. Laser | And, in 1970, Bell Labs invented a special kind of laser that is likely to have as great an effect on our civilization as the transistor did. Believe it or not, that little white cube on the left of your screen is a crystal of salt. But, I'd like to save that for a moment and talk a little bit more about today . . . what's happening right now. |
| #58. ESS | Remember that transistor Bell Labs invented back in 1947? Well, it's enable the Bell System to develop an electronic switching system, called ESS, that's faster, quieter and more efficient than any switching system we've ever had before. |

**Fig. 4—This is also what a television news script looks like. "Audio," or what you read, is on the right-hand side of the page. "Video," or what the audience sees, is on the left-hand side of the page. The "video" side is used for visual instructions—slide number, roll film, etc.**

techniques of a nonvisual speech—stand erect and face the audience, give them as much eye contact as possible. Once you hit your first slide, you should shift your body slightly in the direction of the screen.

In effect, what you are saying to your audience without words is: "Let's look at these pictures together." From that point on, concentrate on the script and the slides, glancing at the audience only where the same slide stays on the screen for a long time—six or seven lines of the script.

Unless it's a very "busy" slide—with a lot of stuff on it to see—the audience will glance at it and then look back at you as you talk. They won't be the least offended if most of your attention is shifting back and forth between your script and the screen.

If something goes wrong with the presentation—a slide skips, or doesn't come up—relax and get it straightened out. With a slide presentation, audiences are usually very patient. Not long ago a friend of mine was giving a slide show to a very powerful group of people, and he noticed that the wrong slide was on the screen. He said out loud, "Now, where did that slide of the telephone go?" Half of the audience shouted out in good humor, "It's two slides back." The rest of the presentation was done with ease, and the speech was a great success.

Everything gets better with practice, and working with slides in a speech becomes easier with each performance. One of the really good things about using slides in a speech is that they tend to take some of the formality and stiffness out of a program. The audience seems to lean back and relax as though they were settling in to watch a movie. By being aware of this mood, the tension for a speaker should also be less.

If your speech lends itself to slides and you have some good ones—use them. They won't hurt, and they may help to make the speech better.

# 3

# Ready, Set, Go

## Ready

IT'S assumption time again. Let's assume that you have a speech. It's written the way you want it. The words say what you want to say (within reason). You've rehearsed it until you are familiar with it, and changed all the phrases and words which are cumbersome or awkward when *spoken*. Now you have received a call; someone wants you to give your speech to their service club, or your boss has asked you to give a speech to an organization. You now have to get ready to give it.

The first thing you should do is call the person who is in charge of the meeting and ask a few questions. What kind of a meeting is it? Do they hold a business session before the speech (or program)? Do they eat before or after—or not at all? What kind of a room will the meeting be held in? What are they expecting from you? Are there going to be any other speakers? What size audience can you expect? What kind of an audience? Are they predominately older or younger, liberal or conservative? What mechanical aids will be available in the meeting room—podium, PA system, lighting? Most important—review the facts. Are you in complete agreement about the location of the meeting, the date of the meeting, the time of day, and the time allotted for your part of the program?

While this check list may sound like one for a pilot about to take off in a jumbo jet with a full load of passengers, it's really not all that bad. It boils down to about a five-minute friendly phone call. Most program chairmen will anticipate your needs and answer all the questions I've listed plus additional information about their clubs.

Armed with this knowledge a week or two before your speaking engagement, you can either leave your speech as it is and relax, or make a few changes if you feel it's necessary—and relax.

You are ready for the big day.

## Set

Getting set to give a speech begins with getting dressed. There have been innumerable surveys taken and articles written about leisure suits and other modern dressing habits. You can find surveys where a vast majority of the people say leisure suits are perfectly acceptable and even more welcome than business suits. Other surveys and articles prove conclusively that people who wear leisure suits don't go very far in management and are not completely trusted with responsibility. I don't care if you are going to speak at a convention of hoboes, in my book, there's only one way for a speaker to dress—for a man, in a suit. For a lady, in a dress or a women's suit. And make sure it's conservative. A man can get by with a sport coat, as long as it doesn't look like he's heading for the race track after his speech. Dress conservatively, and here's why. One of the very first things anybody who teaches public speaking will tell you is, "Don't distract the audience by jangling keys or scratching your nose." A big deal is made out of all these distracting habits of some speakers. Well, the biggest *first* distraction of all is the clothes we wear. Put any label on it you want, "first impressions," "clothes make the man," et cetera, the fact is, clothes are the first thing we see in others. Most famous people have been asked, "What is the first thing you notice in a girl or a guy?" And their answers are always, "I noticed their eyes." Or, "I noticed their legs or their hands or their nose or their teeth." And that may all be very true *if—if* the person being noticed is wearing normal clothing. But if they are dressed outlandishly, the first thing noticed will be their clothes. And that's exactly what a speaker does *not* want noticed—his or her clothing. Seventy percent of an audience, or whatever percentage those who favor leisure suits are coming up with, may not be bothered by a speaker in a leisure suit. But that means 30 percent of the audience will be distracted, at least for the first few, important minutes of the speech, by the speaker's clothing. Odd clothes can be just as distracting as jangling keys or irritating mannerisms, such as scratching your nose (to put it politely). So, why take the chance? Dress conservatively.

Clarence Darrow gave some pretty good courtroom speeches in rolled up shirt sleeves, but most of us are not Clarence Darrow.

So much for clothes. The day has arrived and you have selected a nice suit or dress (something comfortable) and head off for your speaking engagement.

Head off early. Plan on arriving at least a half hour before anyone else is due on the scene. Ninety percent of your speeches will be given in restaurants, hotels, auditoriums, or other public places where you will be able to look over the facilities before the crowd arrives. Use this half hour to make sure there is a podium, proper lighting, PA system (if needed), electrical outlets (if you are using slides), or anything else you deem necessary for your talk. Watch that lighting. One time I was giving a speech at an annual banquet as part of a program that included several other events prior to my comments. I was fully prepared and checked everything out, I thought. The podium was there, microphone—everything was perfect. The banquet was held in a restaurant which overlooked a lake and had great, big windows for taking advantage of the view. It was late spring and at 6:30 in the evening there was plenty of light. At 7:30, as we were enjoying our meal, there was still plenty of light. At 8:30, when the master of ceremonies was handing out awards and taking care of other miscellaneous business, the light was beginning to fade. By the time I got up to speak at 9 p.m., the dim lights which made it easy for diners to look out at the activity on the lake and the city lights on the far shore were completely inadequate for me to see my script. Anti-scripters would argue, "See, if you had memorized your speech, it wouldn't have made any difference." That's true, it would have been just as bad as it was. On the other hand, if I had thought about the sun fading away, I would have made sure that there would be a podium light, and the speech would have gone off as planned.

Arrive a half hour early and let there be light!

By arriving early, you will be putting the program chairman at ease and this will result in a happy relationship. He'll help you with any arrangements, and it will give you an opportunity to discuss your introduction, name pronunciations—yours and his or whoever it is who will be introducing you—and give you time to adjust to any last minute alterations in the program.

Podiums. I keep mentioning them because they are important. Not only do they hold your script and keep it out of sight, but they give you something to hang onto, so that your hands won't shake. And, if you are not the nervous type, they provide a dignified place to put your hands so that they don't end up in your pockets, behind your back, or across your chest a la Il Duce. Placing your hands on a podium seems to lend authority and presence to a speaker. But, podiums can also cause problems for speakers if they are too short or too high for the speaker. By arriving early, you can correct this problem. One time, when I was about to give a speech to a large Shriner luncheon, I noticed the podium was on a base no more than 2 or 3 inches high and placed on the luncheon table. When I read speeches, I wear glasses. But, on that podium my script would have been so far away I would have needed binoculars to see the words. A quick trip to the kitchen turned up a big, plastic basin used to carry dirty dishes from the tables. I put it under the podium and it worked out just fine, not only for me, but for everyone else as well. Some short speakers ask to have a box placed behind the lecturn for them to stand on.

One final word for getting "set" before you "go" on with the speech.

Don't eat too heavily, and stay away from mucous-causing drinks such as coke or milk. Water is your best bet. Listen attentively to all the other speakers. There are always other speakers, the club president getting in his word, the chairman of the flower committee, and so on. By listening to them, you not only pick up a possible comment or two that you can use while adjusting your microphone (coming up), but, also the audience will see that you are not a self-centered person interested only in your own words.

## Go

Are you nervous? Let me tell you a quick story that incorporates almost everything I've said about speeches and scripts. As I'm writing these words, I feel great because of a speech I gave last night before the city council of the town where I live. It's a bedroom community of about 80,000 people and my son is a Little League ball player. Last week, the presidents of the Little Leagues in this community asked me to go before the city council to argue against a park department plan to charge for using the ball fields in the city parks. I knocked off a five-minute speech giving our arguments why there should be no charge, and then I gave it in front of the mayor, the city manager, five councilmen, the park department head, other city officials, and about 50 people in the council chamber. This morning, both the local paper and the city newspaper carried the story with our arguments. This evening, the park department rescinded its order, and the kids will be able to use the ball fields free. But, last night, a half hour before getting up and making an impassioned plea, my heart was pounding and my hands were sweating. I had never before given this kind of a speech. But, I put that script on the podium and started to read. I knew the speech was good because I had shown it to a half dozen Little League officials for their approval, and they said it was good. Before a minute of the presentation had gone by, my nervousness was gone, and I was making eye contact with each member of the city council, the mayor, and the city manager. By the time five minutes had gone by, I was sorry the speech was ending. I felt like I could have kept talking for an hour.

Was it the speech that changed the minds of the city officials? Who knows? One thing for sure, without it, or something like it, nothing would have happened. The speech plus copies handed to the press produced results—positive and quick. The point is—I was really scared. But, because I had a script, I knew the worst thing that could happen would be that I would stare at the script and just read the words. I knew that I would not forget what I came to say because it was all there in front of me. I also knew, before reading one word, that sometime before I finished reading the script the nervousness would be gone—I just didn't know how long it would take. It took about thirty seconds.

There are all kinds of stories about the gimmicks famous people have used to get over nervousness— they think of the audience sitting out there naked, or with only their shorts on, or holes in their socks. If you think that will help, by all means, *do it.* Frankly, I think the best thing you can think of is all the other speakers you have heard who have gotten up before an audience and stammered, hemmed and hawed, and digressed as they stared at the ceiling while they tried to think about what they were going to say next. Think about that, and you will be much more confident with your script.

Are you nervous? You'll get over it. Now, let's "go."

Acknowledge your introduction by using the name of the person who introduced you. This is a good time to take care of the microphone. Microphones never seem to be adjusted properly for speakers, and now, before you get into your prepared speech, is the time to make these adjustments. As you are acknowledging people at the head table or commenting on something that happened just before you got up to the podium, get the mike into a position about 6 inches away from your mouth. If it looks like there is a sound problem, come right out and ask the audience if they can hear you. Do all of this *before* you get into your speech.

Once you begin to speak, don't worry about mistakes. Remember that radio and TV announcers and newsmen stumble over words. They're pros—but they don't apologize, they just continue. So should you. If you are using slides and they come out upside down or other mechanical things go wrong, such as a pulled plug or a light burning out, keep in mind that these things happen and everybody knows they happen. It's only embarrassing if you make it so.

Don't rush your speech.

If it's a good speech and you read it just reasonably well, you'll be a success.

# 4

# Questions and Answers

THE FIRST TIME the word "shill" floated into my ears was back in 1953. I was 22 years old and on my way to San Francisco from Richmond, Virginia. A broken rear window in my car, which couldn't be replaced immediately in Kingman, Arizona, gave me an excuse to detour from Route 66 and spend the night in Las Vegas, Nevada.

During this brief visit I was introduced to the game of chance called "21" and learned how to tell the difference between the customer and a houseman.

Casino operators believe it is bad business for a dealer to stand behind a "21" table without several people sitting in front of it making bets. To avoid this barren scene, they hire people (usually down and out gamblers) and pay them poorly to pretend they are high rollers. This takes a lot of pretending considering the hired bettors are only given ten silver dollars when they sit down and aren't allowed to bet more than a dollar at a time. But they fooled me, since I was only betting 50 cents in those days. In time, I learned these hired hands are called shills.

In opera, being a bit higher-class, they're called claques, taken from the French meaning to clap, or applaud. Opera singers hire claques to clap at appropriate times, and this encourages the rest of the audience to applaud when the singer finishes an aria.

During the question and answer period following a speech, I have seen versions of shills and claques ask questions when things begin to lag or to help get something started; they're called friends, secretaries, or assistants. There's nothing wrong with doing this, but in case you don't have a secretary or assistant with you, you can accomplish the same result by asking some "self" questions; such as—"I'm often asked. . ." or "The other day someone asked me. . . ." If you go through two or three self questions and answers and still don't get a query from the audience, thank them for listening to your speech and go home. But, if the audience does start asking questions, it helps a lot to know how to answer them. So, if you are passing yourself off as well-informed on the subject of your speech, make sure you are.

The question and answer period, according to most speech experts—and on this I fully concur—can be one of the most fruitful parts of your presentation. Research studies show a high interest, motivation, and improved attitude toward the speaker, his company, and his message developing from the Q & A part of the program. Don't pass it up if the situation allows time for it.

Before the meeting, make arrangements with the program chairman on who will manage the questions. In a small group it is better to manage it yourself to avoid stepping on each other's toes. In a larger group the program chairman can keep an eye out for hands while you are answering questions. In small groups it's usually not necessary to repeat questions and, in fact, can be irritating. However, if it's a larger group and the person asking the question is sitting down front and you doubt if others in the audience heard the question, then repeat the question. This judgment should be in your hands.

## Answering Questions

These answering techniques will help you answer questions in a simple and easy to understand way. None of the techniques is an attempt to manipulate or mislead the questioners. I strongly advise against any kind of deception.

1. Always tell the truth. First, it's only right, and any attempt to do otherwise works to destroy your credibility.

2. In answering a question, be brief and to the point. Enlarge on the subject or supply additional information if this is called for, but don't start a chain reaction yourself by going from the point of the question to a series of other points.

3. If a questioner tries to interrupt you before you have finished your response, pause and let him finish, then continue your answer. Don't let yourself be drawn into the position of talking louder than him just to be heard. If he persists in interrupting, don't get into an argument, but do insist on the right to give a complete answer. In most cases the audience will recognize his rudeness.

4. If asked several questions at once, or hit with several false premises in a question, don't let this get by.

For example, "Why is it that at a time when your service is a mess and your company is making unprecedented profits, you are laying people off right and left?"

You might reply: "Well, you raised several questions there. Let me respond to your main point first . . . ."

5. Avoid company language and abbreviations. There is no such thing as a "widget consumer" (someone who eats widgets?); "integrated manufacturing" today can well mean blacks and whites working side by side; an "operating company" sounds a little sinister.

6. Don't let others put words in your mouth. It's a good policy to answer all questions that start, "Do you mean to say . . ." with a clear, concise statement of what *you do* mean to say.

7. If a questioner wants information you can't release because of company policy, don't be evasive. Tell him matter-of-factly and without resentment that you can't release it. If you can explain why the information is being withheld without getting into the specifics you want to avoid, do so. For example, "We do not permit pictures or release names and addresses of management people working during strikes, because such action could result in danger to employees who are working night and day to provide you with service."

8. Don't be afraid to say, "I don't know." But do it positively. For example, "Our company services thousands of people in different parts of the state, and I'm simply not exposed to all the many different service offerings. But, I'll get that answer to you if you'll give me your address or phone number after the meeting."

## Some General Guidelines

- Listen to each question very carefully.
- Try not to rely on "canned" procedures for introducing your answer (e.g., "That's a good question"—especially when it isn't); approach your answer carefully and honestly.
- Don't make rash promises (e.g. "I'll solve that problem for you").

- Don't allow one or two persons to monopolize the Q & A period; encourage many to participate.

### Recognize the Nature of the Question

Remember that there are three types of questions: neutral, friendly, or hostile. A neutral question is usually a simple request for information: "Are the food processors in the Northwest in danger of going out of business?"

A friendly question usually betrays a bias: "I know the food processors are in danger of going out of business in the Northwest—what can be done about it?"

A hostile question would sound like this: "Do you really think people are going to buy that line about going out of business when you're making so much money?"

The neutral and friendly questions can be answered by stating some facts. The hostile question may be prefaced with a statement such as: "I don't know whether people will accept the facts, I can only present them . . . ." Then give the facts.

The main point when answering hostile questions is to remain calm and avoid being dragged into an argument.

## Hecklers

If it weren't for hecklers, some comedians, such as Don Rickles, wouldn't be in business. George Bernard Shaw always felt superior to hecklers and looked forward to their comments as a source of amusing interchange. A man in the audience once shouted at Shaw, "Come, Shaw, you know all this stuff is balderdash."

Shaw answered, "I quite agree with you, my

friend, but who are you and I against so many?"

There is no perfect defense against heckling except making sure that your facts are correct. Never get angry or exchange bitter words with a heckler. The chances of running into a heckler at an audience to which you have been invited to speak are very rare. If you should encounter one, keep your "cool," and the chances are excellent that the audience will come over to your side.

## When To Wrap It Up

When the time for questions is up or when the questons stop, whichever comes sooner (most programs have a set time for ending), the speaker should draw the meeting to a fitting close.

If there is no set time for the program to end, the speaker should watch for cues from the audience that the program has lasted long enough. If a few people seem anxious to leave but others wish to continue the question period, the speaker should graciously announce that some members may have to leave and should feel free to at any time. It is not enough to say rather weakly, "Well, I guess that's it." Neither is it appropriate to say nothing. A fitting close requires the speaker to thank the audience for listening and restate the theme of his message. For example, he might say "I thank you for giving me the opportunity to tell you about some of the things my company is doing to improve communications between you and your neighbors across the country."

Naturally, the audience, through applause, should thank the speaker for being their guest, but it is *never wrong* for the speaker to thank the audience for the opportunity to speak. Whether he thanks the audience or not, the speaker should be certain not to let the program fade away at the close of the question and answer period. A speaker should maintain control of the communication setting until the final applause.

# 5

# Clients
# Question Me

No MATTER how well a speech is prepared to anticipate audience questions, they still come. You should always leave enough time at the end of a speech to answer questions. I follow this advice myself when giving speeches, and in classroom situations I allow plenty of time between instructing and video-taping for questions. And, just like speeches, no matter how well prepared the material is, there are always plenty of questions.

After a time, I began to take notes of these classroom questions and decided to use the Q & A format as a way to cover a lot of material in this book about speeches without getting into a "puff" job. After all, if you want to know whether to type your speech in upper or lower case, it doesn't require a whole chapter for an answer. Entire books have been written on voice exercises and breath control, but only opera singers really need to read about, practice, and absorb the hundreds of different techniques for developing a 5-octave voice and the ability to hold a note for 15 minutes.

One or two easy-to-follow, daily exercises you can do almost anywhere, any time, and without interfering with a normal routine, offer a much more practical approach.

One question I am asked often—and it almost prompted a separate section for this book—is: "I've spent $20,000 to learn how to give a speech and I didn't learn a damn thing. I'd still like to learn how to give a speech, but I don't want to get ripped off. How can I avoid it?" Well, that's a pretty long question and the answer could also be stretched out to a whole chapter I could call "The Hustlers." But I decided to put one or two examples in this section rather than dwell on it. And rather than dwell anymore on explaining this format, let's get on with the questions, starting with:

*Question:* Should I use upper or lower case when having my speech typed?

*Answer:* By using lower case, what you see on your script will be what you normally see when reading your newspaper, a book, and almost anything else you read. A speech script typed entirely in upper case could add an unnecessary handicap to your out-loud reading capability. The main reason for upper case typing is to provide larger print and consequently make the script easier to see. I recommend always using lower case. If your eyes are too weak to see the script clearly, wear glasses.

*Question:* Your suggestion to use wide margins and half-pages for a script is fine, except for one thing: what do I do when I have a long speech and find the script is too thick for the "lip" of the podium to hold?

*Answer:* If your script is too thick, place a block of wood on the lip of the podium. This will not only hold your script but has the additional advantage of pushing the script higher on the podium, and as noted earlier, the higher a script is on the podium, the

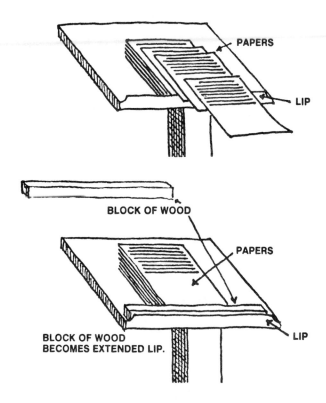

**Fig. 5—A one-inch square block of wood placed on the lip of a podium not only retains a thicker script to rest securely on the podium, it also pushes the script higher on the podium permitting better eye contact.**

better your eye contact and the easier it is to read.

*Question:* I notice that many "important" speakers take off their watches and place them on the side of the podium before they start speaking. Should I do that?

*Answer:* If you're not using a script, putting your watch on the podium is better than constantly lifting your wrist into the air to look at the time. However, there's a bad implication attached to "clock-watching." How would you feel if you were in a conversation with someone and he kept glancing at his watch? I never worry about time when giving a speech because I know by my script exactly how long it's going to be before I start. With some exceptions, such as the late Walter Winchell, most people speak at a rate of between 130 and 140 words a minute. If you are asked to give a ten-minute speech, you'll need a script of about 1,400 words. A 20-minute speech—2,800 words. If a program is 30 minutes long and you get "on" 5 minutes late with your 20-minute speech, you'll know you must limit questions to 5 minutes or end a few minutes earlier without short-changing the audience.

*Question:* What if there is no podium at the place where I'm supposed to speak? What do I do with my script in that case?

*Answer:* That happened to me a few times when I first started speaking to groups. So, I designed a portable podium I always carry in the trunk of my car. It's made of heavy wood and, when folded, looks like a brief case. When unfolded, it works out beautifully on any table, including a card table, if necessary, in a private home. Since then I have learned that several companies make portable podiums, some of them very elaborate with built-in mikes, speakers, and lights. Others are flimsily made. If you are uncertain about the availability of a podium where you'll be speaking, carry one in your car. Arrive for your speaking engagement ahead of time; if there is no podium, return to your car and bring your own to the speaker's platform.

*Question:* Should I join the Toastmasters?

*Answer:* If you are a complete novice, the right Toastmasters Club can be very helpful. For one thing, it will give you a chance to get up before an audience on a regular basis and give a speech—and there's nothing like experience. However, you should be warned of a couple of pitfalls. Each Toastmasters Club has its own personality—some are good and some are bad. Part of the benefit of belonging to Toastmasters is the criticism leveled by the rest of the members whenever you give a speech. Unfortunately, the criticism at times can be harsh and even unwarranted, and there's nothing a speaker needs less than unwarranted, wrong, and ego-deflating criticism. Another fault with Toastmasters, in my opinion, is too much stress on memorization and gimmickry rather than the speech itself and the delivery of it. I would suggest trying out a couple of different Toastmaster Clubs and see how it works out. If you enjoy it—great. If not, get out.

*Question:* You said many people listen to speeches, yet you write about audiences of 20 or 30 people. What good would it do my company to establish a speakers bureau and then reach only small audiences?

*Answer:* Ohio Bell's speakers bureau of 250 employees give speeches on their own time. In 1975 members of Ohio Bell Speaker's Bureau spoke to 100,030 people. Assuming that those in the audiences told their spouses something about the speech, as many as 200,000 people received all or part of the phone company's message. A Pacific Northwest Bell manager in a small eastern Washington town completed his speakers bureau training in March of 1977 and gave his first speech to 21 people in April. Almost all of his speech was printed in the local newspaper, which has a circulation of 6,000.

*Question:* I have a slight accent. Should I take diction lessons to get rid of it?

*Answer:* That's up to you, but first, ask yourself— Has anyone complained about the accent? Although you don't hear many in broadcasting, an accent can be a bonus for a speaker. Think back to the last eight

Presidents of the United States. Roosevelt and Kennedy (and now Carter) spoke with noticeable accents and were considered to be the best of our Presidential speakers in the past 50 years. Truman, Eisenhower, Nixon, and Ford had no pronounced accents but were less effective speakers. (LBJ was also less effective—even though he had an accent.) I don't think an accent matters.

*Question:* I can't buy your argument about conservative clothing. Aren't leisure suits perfectly acceptable today?

*Answer:* Maybe, but clothing is more important than many people would like to believe. A 6-year study of two identical groups of male managers showed that businessmen wearing computer-selected clothing earned $4,000 a year more than their counterparts, held better positions, and were more enthusiastic about their work. I don't know how computers dressed those men, but the successful businessmen I know dress on the conservative side. Use your own judgment. If you are 23 and speaking to a group about the drug culture and "your experiences with it," a business suit might be out of place. For most men, and for almost all speaking engagements, a business suit is seldom wrong, but a leisure suit could be. Why take a chance?

*Question:* You said that for newspapers, television, or radio, leaders have a tendency to pull their punches when presenting a message, but for specific groups, a person can gear a speech to the audience. If a speech is geared to the audience, isn't that the same as pulling punches?

*Answer:* A couple of examples will answer this question. A business client of mine was so conservative he would have had to move to the left to get a right wing label. His position as manager of an all-news radio station prompted a Democratic Club to invite him to give a speech on news. He gave the speech without compromising his position one iota, made the points that needed to be made, and received a standing ovation. True, he didn't reveal *all* his beliefs, but he did cover a particularly important area, and he made friends and listeners for his station.

Another client, a well-known labor leader and Democrat, wrangled an invitation to speak to a Republican Club whose members were, for the most part, even more conservative than the radio station manager. This labor leader didn't talk about unions or strikes. Instead he talked about the government bureaucracy, calling the higher echelon employees and appointees of government, "New Mandarins." The Republicans loved it. So did a dozen other audiences ranging from working people to general service clubs. And, he never said anything he didn't believe. However, both of these speakers slanted their speeches for different audiences. The basic speeches remained the same, but before a businessman's audience, the labor leader would say, "These bureaucrats are strangling the free enterprise system and killing the small businessman with taxes." Before a labor audience he would say, "These bureaucrats are strangling the working man and taxing him to death with their schemes to gain power for themselves."

The labor leader, although he hated big business, really considered the small businessman in the same category as other workers. By lauding "free enterprise" and "small business," he appealed to conservative audiences. By switching to the "workingman," he appealed to labor audiences. His speech, which remained basically the same, was geared to "specific" audiences. He didn't have to pull his punches.

*Question:* My voice isn't very good. What can I do to improve it?

*Answer:* Whenever some guy opens his mouth and large, sonorous tones come out sounding as if they were coming from his toes, we may envy his voice. But, short of stridency, pronounced nasalness, or a serious speech impediment, what we sound like is part of our personality, and I wouldn't get too excited about making any drastic changes. As an occasional speaker and for every-day conversation, try to improve your resonance and tone quality just for the sake of improvement, self-satisfaction, and to be better understood when giving a speech. Daily humming helps to improve your voice quality. That's right—humming. For dramatic improvements in your voice, a good voice teacher can be very helpful—mine was. Books loaded with voice exercises are available. But, like any other exercise, you must determine how much of a sacrifice you want to make. I've never had a student whose voice was so bad that I would recommend anything more than humming and a little "toot, toot, toot" exercise. The "toot-toot" is impossible to explain—it has to be demonstrated in all of its ridiculousness. Try humming.

*Question:* Should I begin every speech by telling some jokes?

*Answer:* Humor, even in a serious speech, relaxes the audience *and* the speaker. But, there's a big difference between humor and telling jokes. Few people are good at telling jokes—I'm not. Jokes should relate to your speech. Too often jokes are dragged into a script, kicking and screaming. If you are really good at telling a short joke and it has some connection to the speech, the occasion , or to yourself, go ahead and tell it.

One speech consultant I know advised his students—"*Never* read a joke or a funny story." I can't go along with that. In all my speeches, jokes, funny stories, and one-liners are written and read. If they weren't written, I'd forget some of the important parts—possibly even the punch line. Have you ever watched Bob Hope reel off his one-liners on television? He's reading them all! Would the cartoons and jokes in magazines be any funnier if, instead of reading them, the average person would tell them to you—possibly leaving out a couple of key words? In any case, humor can add balance to a speech if used properly and sparingly. But, observe these definite rules: stay away from off-color and poor taste humor such as ethnic jokes and stories. Never start off with an apology— "I'm not very good at telling jokes, but . . ." Never make yourself the hero of a story. At the beginning of the speech, the first page or two can be filled with humor, but thereafter it should be used sparingly.

*Question:* Is there anything else, besides what you mentioned earlier, that can help alleviate nervousness when I'm giving a speech?

*Answer:* Jimmy Carter was once asked if he wasn't awed by the prospect of becoming President. He replied: "When I compare myself to the Presidency as an office, I feel inadequate. When I compare myself to others who might be there instead of me, I feel adequate." When I am asked to give a speech, I feel honored but inadequate. When I think of other speakers I have heard, I don't feel so inadequate. Of course, always try to think of the bad speakers you've heard—not that pro who had them rolling in the aisles and cheering at the end.

*Question:* I seem to run "out of gas" about halfway through a script speech. What can be done about that?

*Answer:* Talking, like anything else we do, uses muscles—diaphragm, throat, tongue, etc. In giving a speech, you also use your eyes, legs, and arms. If you ever watched a baseball game, you probably noticed the batter, before going to the plate, will either swing two or three bats a few times or a bat with a batting ring (a heavy weight) on it. Just before stepping into the box, he'll remove the weight from his bat. The idea behind this is to make the bat seem lighter (which it is in comparison to three bats or a weight) and easier to swing. If you have the problem of running out of gas halfway through a speech, I recommend reading the speech twice without stopping the day before you give it. You will become more familiar with the script and develop your muscles—the actual performance will seem lighter—easier.

*Question:* Should I speak to, at, or with an audience?

*Answer:* Wow! I keep hearing about those three different techniques, but I'm not sure I know exactly what they mean. Talking at an audience may translate into talking down to people—arms folded across the chest, no eye contact, perhaps an arrogant stance. I don't think you'd want to do that. Talking with an audience can best be described by recalling the technique of Will Rogers. His technique requires a lot of skill and talent that most of us lack. It also can make you look foolish, if it doesn't come off, by destroying your authority or dignity. Talking to an audience doesn't require a great deal of eye contact or intimacy, but it *does* require a good speech. I always try to have a good speech and talk to an audience during the speech and a little talking with the audience during questions and answers. Frankly, with a good speech read from a script, this question answers itself.

*Question:* If I use a script, how can I read the reaction of the audience to my speech and make the necessary changes if I appear to be losing them?

*Answer:* This could come under the heading of body-English, or, in scientific terms, kinesis. For a quick answer, *don't* try to read the reaction of your audience while you're giving a speech. *Don't* try to change the speech in the middle of it. To begin with, unless the audience starts throwing tomatoes at you, it's almost impossible to tell what the people are thinking. And, if they do start throwing tomatoes, you'd better change your location instead of the speech.

I realize that many speech instructors emphasize "reading" the audience and then making adjustments to your talk if it doesn't seem to be getting the right reception. I think this is dumb. As a matter of fact, I'm not so sure that kinesis isn't dumb. Since so much is made out of reading an audience, let's look at the science of body-English for a moment to see how it applies to speeches. One London-based management consultant has evaluated thousands of managers by reading what they *don't* say. His interview assessments are about two hours long and are based on everything *but* the word content. Here's an example: The open-and-up-turned palms shrug is such a blatant "I have nothing to hide" gesture, it usually hides something. In other words, when my wife asks me when I expect to finish this book and I shrug with my palms up and say, "Darned if I know," because I don't know, then I'm supposed to be hiding something. Baloney! Obviously, for a deaf-mute, body language, or sign language, is practically the whole ball game. For the rest of us, ever since mankind started to form words and to give those words meaning, the goal has been to communicate with words—written and spoken. A word was even given to that ability—literacy. For those who couldn't communicate by either the spoken or written word, another word was coined—illiterate.

I can't resist quoting one sentence I came across in a college textbook about communications and body language. This is from *Reader in Public Opinion and*

*Communications*, Second Edition, Berelson and Jano-
witz (New York Free Press). At the bottom of page 160
it says:

"Conscious communication—conscious conversation of gestures—arises when gestures become signs,
that is, when they come to carry for the individuals
making them and the individuals responding to them,
definite meanings or significations in terms of the
subsequent behavior of the individuals making them,
they make possible the mutual adjustments of the
various components of the social act to one another,
and also, by calling forth explicitly in the individuals
to whom they are made, they render possible the rise
of self-consciousness in connection with this mutual
adjustment."

Now I ask you, what the hell does all that mean?
If this one sentence—yes, it is just one sentence—is
what body language is all about, I think I'll try to keep
fumbling along with the spoken word. That one sentence reads like a bank's annual report. Of course,
when a guy and a gal get together alone and romanti-
cally, words can get in the way. It helps to be able to
read eyes and sighs. Even though a speaker might be
trying to "woo" an audience, however, trying to read
something into eyes and sighs is generally a waste
of time.

Here are just two examples that I use in my
classes. Once I was giving a speech to a large crowd
of very elderly gentlemen who looked like they either
died or fell asleep after my first few words. My reaction to those bowed heads in the audience was just
short of panic; I was tempted to stop talking and go
home. But, since I was already there, I thought that
I might as well press on and finish the speech. I'm
glad I did. At the end, half of the audience rushed to
the head table and threw dollar bills on it, asking if
they could buy a copy of the speech. They loved it.

Afterward, I analyzed the situation and came to the conclusion that these nice old geezers had a good lunch and had simply settled back to listen to what I had to say. A few of them leaned forward with their heads in their arms, which were resting on the table. That was their way of listening. But if I had followed the advice of those who say, "Look at the audience and if they're not paying attention and hanging onto every word you utter, change your speech," I would have made a horrible mistake.

Another time I was giving a rather controversial speech about broadcast news. One guy in the front row kept looking at me with a glare that can only be described as sheer belligerence. I kept avoiding his eyes as much as possible and hoping that I could get out of the place afterward without his pounding my head into the podium. As it turned out during questions and answers, he agreed with almost everything I said, enjoyed the talk, and later became a fan of mine. He just happened to be one of those people who looks mean when they're listening closely.

To answer the question again—how do you "read" an audience? Don't try. Don't think your speech is boring because a few members of the audience look like they're falling asleep. When you're through, they are likely to be the first to the podium to congratulate you and to be the most enthusiastic recipients of your message. Conversely, the attentive-looking man or lady with the big smile might very well be storing up questions for cutting you apart when you're finished. You can generally "feel" when your speech is going exceptionally well, but you will often be surprised at how well it has been received when you thought it was going badly.

*Question:* How can I keep from getting "ripped off" by speech coaches or ghost writers?

*Answer:* If you've ever watched a Little League

coach training his young charges, the word you'll hear more than any other is "hustle." A baseball player who is a hustler is the right kind of player to have on your team. This is generally true in business, also. It's the American Way. Get out there and hustle—be a hustler! So, it's pretty hard to knock hustlers. On the other hand, none of us wants to be hustled out of our money without getting something in return. In the past few years, communications "experts" have sprung up all over the country. The real expertise of many of these people, however, is not in teaching communications, but in extracting large contracts from companies to razzle dazzle them without the company gaining much from the big bucks that are spent. Example:

There's the case of the college speech professor who moonlights by teaching company executives in his area how to give speeches. For a bunch of bucks, he meets with the same executives once or twice a month for a couple of years. According to one of my friends, who was one of those executives, the prof spent most of his time insulting the students or standing around talking and drinking coffee. His very long course, of which I happen to have a copy, consists mainly of material lifted from other professors or famous speakers. Did the course do any good? Even an idiot will learn something if he's been exposed to it for a couple of years. Was it worth the money spent? Well, it's a big company and it's all tax deductible, but in my opinion, it was money thrown away.

Then there's the case of a big city-owned utility company. Someone in the utility hierarchy decided the personnel should learn how to deal with the news media and go out and give speeches. So, they hired a charming, high-powered young man from Texas to teach them. The fee: $120,000. To make a long, sad story short, his methods didn't work very well. How do I know? Because when the expert from Texas got through, the utility went out and hired a knowledgeable friend of mine to teach their people how to give speeches. The only problem was that he had never taught anyone how to give a speech. He didn't tell them. Instead, he came to me. I gave him a quickie course on how to give a quickie course, and between the two of us (I helped him with the classes also), those utility people learned how to give speeches.

Your first move in avoiding the "hustlers" is to get rid of any idea that just because a company is big and charges big dollars, it can guarantee big writers or instructors. Once you've gotten "bigness equals quality" out of your mind, the rest is simple. Ask the writer or teaching consultant you plan on hiring for names of other clients you can call. This is important; if they give you the names of other advertising or public relations people, don't accept them as "ability" references. Try to get the name of the person who actually gave the ghost-written speech and the names of the actual people who were coached by the consultant. Then call them and ask: "Was the speech any good? Was the price right? Was the speech-coaching worth the price? More than worth it?" If you get a positive answer from *everybody* you call, you have probably found the right person for the job. In looking for a writer, keep in mind that he may have a flop every now and then. But, a good writer should hit on 9 out of 10 speeches, and the tenth one should be adequate. Also, if at all possible, have the writer read the speech to you the first time you hear it. Don't ask him to drop it off for you to read silently to yourself.

In looking for a speech coach or consultant for yourself or for the people in your company, watch out for those long-term contracts to teach the same people. Almost any intelligent person who wants to learn can be taught—in class sizes of four to six—to give a speech in three days. Some follow-up critiquing and tips after observing the student at a couple of actual speaking engagements can be very helpful. But, at the end of a couple of days of training, most people should know all they need to know to go out and give speeches, and to continue improving by practicing what they learned. Consultants who say they have to work on the same people every month for two years before positive results are reached are looking for steady income from the same person or company.

Let's summarize on how you keep from getting taken:

1. Don't get locked into big names.

2. Call at least three people who used the services of the ghost-writer or speech consultant. Don't accept the names of other consultants or other PR people as references, although they may be helpful in finding out who is available for writing and teaching.

3. Stay away from speech coaches who say they need a year or two to teach someone how to give a speech.

4. Most good writers and teachers are lousy salesmen. If you're being sold by a smooth, fast-talker, watch out.

# II
# News Media

# The News Media
# and Your Speech

Edwin NEWMAN, NBC newsman, doesn't like the term "news media." He contends that media is plural for medium and there are all kinds of media—language, money, CB radio, or people who transmit messages from the departed to the demented. "By themselves," Newman says, "they are inert. Money makes no decisions of its own . . . people in the news business make decisions constantly, and if they amount to nothing more than throwing press releases into the waste basket, that is still significant."

Rather than continue with Ed Newman's words, let it be noted that one of the foremost newsmen of our time is opposed to labeling the news business as news media. Being considerably less erudite than Ed Newman and probably, for that reason, more flexible than he when it comes to terminology, I'll just go ahead and use the phrase "news media" in the same context as just about everyone else.

For if most people working in the news business

want to think of themselves as being in the news media, highly paid publicists dealing with news personnel are Media Specialists, and those who purchase advertising directly or indirectly sponsoring news activities are termed Media Buyers, that's okay with me.

I'm not trying to change jargon that everyone understands, only the esoteric when it's used in public speeches. Aside from personal satisfaction, the main reason for giving a speech at all is to get your ideas across to as many people as possible. That's not easy to do if your audience can't understand the terms, acronyms, and inside trade lingo you use.

In this section it is my intent to look at another way to reach as many people as possible through speeches. As noted earlier, speeches can reach far greater audiences than those present at the time they are given. Speeches can, and often are, printed, reprinted, mailed to people, quoted and misquoted. Portions of speeches even come down to us in history books.

But most people would rather see their words and thoughts get immediate attention rather than wait for the possibility of a posthumous blurb as the "Quote of the Month" in the *Rotarian* magazine.

Getting immediate, far-reaching attention requires news coverage. Therein lies the rub. How does one get good news coverage short of committing a major crime? If I had the answer to that question, I could get rich. No one can guarantee anyone else consistently good news coverage all the time. But certain procedures and techniques can and should be followed to gain the best news coverage possible. These include knowing how to write a news release, set up a news conference, and the exact way to cross your fingers to invoke supernatural powers assuring that the editor won't toss your release into the waste basket with all the rest of the hundreds of news releases that cross his desk each day.*

A good rapport between your public relations department and the news media can be a bridge between your message and the public. It can determine not only whether your message is heard but also *how* it is heard. The failure of business, labor, and government to develop good rapport with the press, however, is not so much the inability of the public relations people to perform their jobs according to the book, but rather their lack of an understanding of the *people* who make up the news media.

Having been a newsman, editor, news director, and commentator for 22 years in small towns and large cities across the nation, it would have been impossible for me not to gather at least a modicum of insight into the feelings of news people, since their problems were my problems, and the lives they live are much like the life I lived. To put it another way, I've walked a mile or two in their shoes.

Knowing how to write a perfect news release without having some knowledge of the nature of news people is like having a Rolls Royce without an engine—it looks great, but it isn't going anywhere. So before getting into the mechanics of news releases

---

*The procedures for news releases and news conferences will be outlined later in this section for the uninitiated. If you find my method too complex, you're welcome to call any print or broadcast editor, and they'll tell you how to do it in 30 seconds. If my methods appear too simple, call any professional public relations firm, and they'll make the whole process of a news release or news conference seem as complicated as open heart surgery—and nearly as expensive. Be warned, however, that big business, big labor, and big government always hire the best public relations people in the nation to write news releases pretty enough to be framed or bound in moroccan leather. Yet, business, government, and labor have seldom come under as many attacks by the news media or held in such low esteem in the eyes of the public as in recent years. Obviously, pretty news releases alone don't do the job.

and news conferences, let's take a brief look at the people who make up the news media—members of the Fourth Estate.

## The Fourth Estate

During the French Revolution ideas were circulated largely by intellectual plebians such as journalists, pamphleteers, and philosophers of the Parisian salons. These writers were sometimes called "The Republic of Letters" and functioned as an extra-constitutional power in the political equation of nobility, clergy, and the common man.

A few years later, in 1828, Thomas Macaulay looked at the balcony in the English Parliament and wrote, "The gallery in which the reporters sit has become a Fourth Estate of the realm." The other three, as in France, were Lords Spiritual, Lords Temporal, and the Commons. In time, the first three estates stood for all government and the fourth estate stood for *any other* influential body in the English political life such as the Army or the press.

Influential may have been an apt term for the fledgling profession of journalism in the mid-nineteenth century, but it would be an understatement today. The news media have emerged in our time as a vastly more potent Fourth Estate—a diverse aggregate of individuals and organizations continuously active in the distribution of information and ideas and even in the shaping of attitudes.

In a paper presented to a meeting of the American Political Science Association, Dartmouth University professor Jeffrey Hart said that around 1960, "We acquired, in effect, a fourth branch of government. The mass media, especially the major networks, but also the major dailies and weekly news magazines, acquired to a larger degree than ever before the capacity to determine the focus of our public debate . . . . The capacity of the media to determine the terms of public debate gives it, at least for extended periods, a political leverage that may be superior to that of a variegated and often ill-informed Congress."

Is the news media as powerful and influential as it's said to be? Well, ask yourself. Even the United States Senate, at the height of its power in the nineteenth century, was unable to get rid of Lincoln's successor, President Andrew Johnson, and he was despised by most of the Senators. No President was ever impeached or left office in midterm except by death. None, that is, until Richard Nixon. The news media not only forced Nixon out of office, they also got rid of his elected Vice President, Spiro Agnew, first.

Now, I'm not passing judgment on the guilt or innocence of Richard Nixon. But the fact is, there have been other Presidents and Vice Presidents in the history of this country who have proven to be less than paragons of strength, virtue, and integrity. They may not have served a second term, but they completed their time in office in spite of the slings and arrows of Congress and the press of earlier eras. The key element is this: Nixon and Agnew would *never* have resigned except for the power and influence of the new Fourth Estate.

Whether Nixon and Agnew should have been pressured out of office in midterm is for history to judge. But, they serve now as examples, and there are many more, to emphasize that the news media have power and can effectively influence, for good or bad, our national life. Napoleon said, "Four hostile newspapers are more to be feared than a thousand bayonets." In the February 19, 1977, issue of *TV Guide,* a series on "Television Today" was begun with a study of news reporting. The conclusion reached: "The medium has power beyond the dreams of conquerors."

Recognition of the news media's awesome strength

has now, as in Napoleon's day, occasioned fear and counterattack. I need not dwell any longer on the force and influence of the Fourth Estate, for it seems everyone else is talking or writing about it. This is particularly true of the business world where almost every day the *Wall Street Journal* or some trade publication features an article on the news media and its newest target, business. On occasion, business will even try to strike back, timidly, and without the slightest effect.

The Fourth Estate is accustomed to being attacked, and vilifying the press is not a new pastime launched by Spiro Agnew in Des Moines, Iowa, in 1969. It dates back at least to 400 B.C. when Plato wrote on government and statesmanship and barely escaped from Sicily with his life.

In America the first newspaper, *Publick Occurrences,* was published in 1690 and was quickly suppressed by government. Thanks to our Constitution, freedom of the press is guaranteed, and ever since the Constitution, criticism of government by the press and the press by government has been accepted and expected. But the press, the News Media, has gained the advantage in this centuries-old battle of seesaw criticism, for it has only been in recent history that the masses of people could read. And today the news audience doesn't even have to do that. News, speculation, and opinion are pumped into minds through radio and television by simply flicking a switch.

With so many more minds to influence, some even illiterate, unquestioning minds, business wonders about a press conspiracy. Now there's a thought that is a favorite topic of spy movies and, as the expression used to go, "little old ladies in tennis shoes."

Is there a conspiracy among news people? The answer is yes and no. Yes, in the sense that they follow a common instinct and that most news comes from a common source. Definitely no, if we're talking about the real meaning of the word—an agreement or design to perform together, conspiring against government, business, or labor.

Actually, the existing situation is far more subtle than a real conspiracy. Secret gatherings have a way of being exposed, and exposure destroys any conspiracy. Instead, we have what I call the "sheep syndrome."

If the network anchorman says business is ripping off the public, the local TV anchorman sagely pronounces that the public is being ripped off by business. If the *New York Times* says the Secretary of State is the Savior of the World, the local reporter thinks the world is being saved by the Secretary of State. In lighter matters, drama and music critics in New York may not reach a consensus on the merits or faults of a new release, but you'll not find a local authority scorning a film they find "perceptive," "sensitive," and a "breakthrough in film expression." The resident movie editor may have been able to make neither heads nor tails of the film, but he'll go on record as liking it.

Even if the local reporter is a kind of maverick trusting his own judgment and not subscribing to the view that all wisdom emanates from the Big Apple or the great society on the Potomac, we're still going to get the opinions of the network reporters or national columnists because a lot of our news comes from the wire services or directly by radio or television from those same sources known as the national press.

To know and understand the Fourth Estate, the very first scrap of knowledge one must have is of the vast difference between the national press corps and the local press. This difference applies not only to scope in news coverage but to people in the news business. Let's begin with coverage. The national press can be generally described as the radio and television networks, the wire services, *Time* and *Newsweek* magazines, and a few newspapers, such as the *New York Times* and the *Washington Post.* Other national newspapers, even those which syndicate, and chain-owned broadcasting companies must be considered local as far as news coverage. So, the one difference between national and local press is the scope of news coverage and the influence wielded by the national group.

The other major difference is the people employed by these two groups. Almost all of the people working for the national press corps, especially for the networks, are extremely well-paid and are among the economic elite of the national work force. Whereas, in the local press—*especially* broadcasters—the reporters are very poorly paid, with the exception of some local anchormen, a few disc jockeys (if they can be considered part of the news media), and a few reporters in the larger cities. In short, the national press corps is extremely well-paid and wields influence nationally, while the local press corps is poorly paid and wields influence locally. That's the only difference between the two groups of people—otherwise, you'll find intelligence and ignorance, arrogance and humility, in both groups.

For most businessmen, it's particularly important to understand the local press corps. Even a giant such as The Boeing Company deals mostly with local reporters. Keep this in mind when we get to the influence that economic conditions have on the local press.*

## The Nature of News and Newsmen

If you think we get a disproportionate amount of

---

*For a good look at the national press corps, see Mel Grayson's book, *The Disaster Lobby* (Follett Publishing Co., Chicago, 1973), and read the chapter, "The Closed Fraternity."

antibusiness or prosocial program news, consider the nature of news itself and the nature of news people. News is not the commonplace. News is still the same old story about the man who bites the dog, not the dog that bites a man.

A factory owner can go along for years paying his employees a fair wage for their work and it's not news. But, let him steal from those people, cheat the government, or get involved in a domestic scandal, and it's a page-one item. Most of the news we see, hear or read is about the seedier, bloodier, and grimier side of life. And, believe it or not, that's the way people want it. A guy in California tried to publish a paper filled with only "good news." It failed dismally.

As for the nature of newsmen, recognize that they are writers of a sort. Writers, whether of news or novels, can be generously categorized as artists. Artists generally lean toward being liberal. So, with few exceptions, newsmen are liberally inclined because they are artistically and intellectually inclined.

It is a fact—most news people are liberal, and they'll usually be the first to admit it. It is also a fact that most Americans are moderates or conservatives. One of the big conflicts in communications, then, is that the people receiving the news are doing so from a moderate or conservative point of view while the people presenting news are doing it from a liberal point of view.

The majority of the news recipients, the audience, no matter how finely tuned their television sets may be, are not completely on the same wavelength as the news presenters. There's bound to be a slight distortion from what is being said and what is being heard.

In addition to the difference of philosophy, there is an attitude among news people bordering on superiority and power coupled with a sense of being exploited. I can remember 25 years ago, when I first went into the broadcasting business, hearing an often repeated phrase. All those people not in the media were referred to as the "unwashed millions."

At the same time they're looking down their noses at us, news people believe that they are grossly underpaid and underappreciated. But, like other businessmen and professionals, they attend conventions and exchange ideas and complaints which result in bonds of mutual interest. Consequently, there's not a cloak and dagger conspiracy against the establishments of government or business; no conspiracy—just a common attitude.

I assume at this point that you are willing to accept the idea that the Fourth Estate is influential and powerful and that there is no covert conspiracy among news people. How, then, can you present your story to the news media? By knowing something about the local press corps!

A northwest utility firm spent $120,000 of tax money to pay a consultant with the expectation that bureaucrats could be taught to communicate. I'm sure they bought a slick package with simulated video tape news conferences, techniques on handling a question and answer period, tips on brightening up news releases, and other gimmicks. Don't get me wrong— these are useful tools. A well-written press release or a professionally conducted news conference can save reporters a lot of time and be helpful to them. But, the company that has its message polished up is still no further ahead if its public relations man is still thought of as a "flack" and he lacks sincerity and understanding. Understanding news people is the first step. Without that, the rest is meaningless gloss.

If you like, call it "knowing your enemy." One thing is certain: if you don't know him, don't expect any breaks. On the other hand, if you do get to know him, that story, which could be balancing on a fine line between making your company look good or bad, has a much better chance of falling on the good side.

Here's an example of how a "friendly" newsman can help a company without slanting, twisting, or doing anything dishonest in reporting the news. Scoop Gotham is a radio reporter in St. Louis and has a good relationship with Trans National Airlines (TNA). Whenever he calls TNA's public relations department for information on a story, the TNA people go all out to assist him in getting the information. When TNA has its annual employee golf outing, they invite Scoop. The relationship is warm, above-board, and there's no "payola" involved. Then, as happened quite often in the fifties and sixties, a TNA plane crashes. Scoop calls the TNA PR department to find out if there were local people aboard and any other information which may help to make his story better than the competition. The PR people are most cooperative with Scoop, and, like every other reporter, he tells the story about the crash including the name of the airline. The name of the airline, particularly for broadcasters, is, for obvious reasons, a vital part of the story on the first day of the crash. The second day, unless there was negligence involved, TNA's name is not vital to every sentence in the story but it still moves on the wire services like this: "That TNA plane crash in the Rockies, which killed 36 people yesterday, has claimed another life. Forty-six-year-old John Smith of Denver died this morning from injuries received in the accident. The TNA airliner was enroute from Chicago to Salt Lake City when a severe electrical storm forced it down. the FAA says there apparently was nothing the TNA pilot could do to avoid the accident." The "friendly" newsman then takes the wire service story and runs a pencil through TNA and the story reads like this: "That plane crash in the Rockies, which killed 36 people yesterday, has claimed another life.

Forty-six-year-old John Smith of Denver died this morning from injuries received in the accident. The airliner was enroute from Chicago to Salt Lake City when a severe electrical storm forced it down. The FAA says there apparently was nothing the pilot could do to avoid the accident."

Now, suppose Scoop's relationship with the TNA PR people is hostile. Every time he calls them for information he's sloughed off or is treated indifferently. He hates TNA. The wire services may very well have sent the story out on the second day without TNA being mentioned or mentioned only once. Scoop takes his pencil and adds TNA into the story as often as he can. He also uses the story, in relation to others of more interest and importance, more often than it deserves for the second day. Every hour on the hour Scoop's listeners hear about the TNA plane crash instead of *a* plane crash. This could go on for a week with every new minor development related to the accident all because a local radio newsman has a strong dislike for the PR department of TNA airlines.

By "knowing" news people, I'm not implying a personal relationship. Most people's circle of acquaintances include one or two people in the media, and the chances are they'll seldom be the ones you can approach with your story. It's also quite possible that even the media people you have met as neighbors, through business, or your local PTA appear much like any of your other acquaintances. But, there are differences, and the big one is when a news person puts on his working clothes.

I've said that most of them have liberal tendencies and that's no crime. It's possible that most people reading this book are liberal. Unlike most people reading this book, however, the average news person in the United States takes home less than $170 a week and faces a job and financial future more precarious than a Boeing engineer in 1970 when the SST was scrapped.

If we can forget about Walter Cronkite and Barbara Walters for a moment, the average reporter makes less money than a garbage collector. Yet, here's a person who is wined and dined at an embassy reception or the governor's mansion, and then goes home and feeds his family peanut butter most of the week to make ends meet.*

The average newsman calling city hall has about as much influence as someone on welfare, maybe less, until he identifies himself as a reporter. Suddenly, he becomes a VIP. There's a great paradox here. A newsman is a low-income working guy with more clout than the owner of a factory. What really makes this struggling, but influential person tick is what's happening in his own environment.

Let's take a hypothetical example.

Jack J. works in the news department of a medium-sized radio or TV station. He has a wife and two children and hopes to be an anchorman at some big TV station by the time his kids are 18. He knows there is no way he'll be able to send them to college on what he makes now as a reporter.

The manager of the station where he works is, in the eyes of J., not too sharp. You'll remember that J. is a newsman, therefore a writer, hence an intellectual, and in his own eyes, brighter than the ordinary boss. But the station manager, who probably came up

*Walt Evans, writing in his *Seattle Times* column of February 9, 1977, puts it this way: "Journalists always have a happy time, right? Easy work, good pay, excitement, adventure. Just last week there was an ad in the classifieds for an editor to edit two weekly newspapers, write a column a week, supervise people, work unusual hours, (including covering night meetings). The position required a darkroom expert, a master's degree, and an international background. High pay? $200 a week. Excitement? In Camas, Washington? Hand me that career guidance book, will you?"

through the ranks of the sales department, is making four to five times as much money as J. The manager is also a businessman.

The people J. talks to on a day-to-day basis are other news persons on his beat or in his newsroom. All his associates have the same problems and the same enemy: management. To compound the problem, every time they call a businessman, they're greeted with suspicion.

Now, what really makes it tough is that J. is a news authority, and whenever he's wearing his news hat on assignment, he is treated like an oracle. Poor J. lives a life you might think came out of Gilbert and Sullivan. With his news hat on, he's a prince, but when it comes off, he's a pauper.

There are compensations. J. gets a lot of free tickets to the circus, ice shows, and sporting events. When he doesn't get the free tickets, he can't afford to go. Worse yet, he may buy tickets for the cheap seats and look down at all the good seats and see businessmen. Maybe they're really plumbers, but they all look like businessmen to J.

Of course, J. picked his own career. For the same cash outlay and mental exertion, he could have obtained a degree in Business Administration. Now, none of this would matter, except for one thing. J. writes the news, and consciously or subconsciously, what he writes is influenced by how he feels. And J. doesn't feel too good about management. That's what I mean about understanding the people in the news media—a lot of them have a chip on their shoulders. Their first grudge is against management which, in their eyes, is business.

There are other factors, of course. One of the big ones I haven't mentioned is the elitism in some quarters of the press. Then there is the influence of the so-called stars, the wire services, liberalism—and *time* is a big enemy. But generally, the local newsman you'll most likely encounter is a counterpart to J. Basically, he is a pretty nice guy. Most of the J's who do those stories putting business in a bad light are not deliberately out to get anyone; it just comes out that way as a result of seeing things from their point of view.

I'm not suggesting that local newsmen are all impoverished; some I've known werc grossly overpaid. And the worst of the advocate journalists are usually the best paid. *They* are the real elitists. But the underpaid, embittered, local newsman is an accurate composite.

To summarize, learning techniques to deal with the news media is helpful, but begin by first learning about the individuals who make up the news media. Out of thousands, there's only one who makes a million dollars a year.

Remember that every business, social, or political program begins with an idea. The idea is circulated until it becomes popular. In business, an idea is developed, and the circulation to make it popular is done though advertising. In social or political programs, the same thing happens: an idea is developed and then circulated—usually through speeches or news—until it becomes popular. You may be inclined to react to news people with a "Who the heck to they think they are?" But when you want to circulate your ideas, when you need the press, or when they go after you, you learn that they do have influence and power. They are called the Fourth Estate, but lately, a lot of people think they might well be called the First Estate.

Now that you know "everything there is to know about local news people," let's turn to the mechanics of news releases and news conferences.

## News Releases

News releases are pieces of paper filled with words that generally come out of the mind and from the pen of a public relations person. Far back in my mind, there's a gnawing feeling that the preceding pages concerning the news media contained a few phrases, such as "flack," that might have left the impression that PR people are about as useful as a snow shovel in Nigeria. Nothing could be further from the truth. The best description of public relations I've heard comes from the PR department of Scandinavian Airlines. To wit: "If a boy meets a girl and tells her how pretty she is, that's *Sales Promotion*. If, instead, he impresses her with how wonderful HE is, that's *Advertising*. But if the girl seeks him out because she has heard from others how splendid a fellow he is, THAT's *Public Relations!*"

One of the problems PR people face is an identity mixup. A lot of the public and, to some degree, news people and corporations have the idea that PR people are press agents and their job is to get publicity for their clients. Good public relations could very well be just the opposite—guiding a company in a manner that it doesn't make the news media.

Robert Fletcher was the PR representative for the Port of Seattle for more than 20 years. Reflecting on those two decades of pouring oil on troubled waters, Fletcher said, "The sad thing about the public relations business is that you very seldom hear the good things. The only way you can tell when the public likes things is when they leave you alone. People never get enough scandal, but they tire of pollyanna stuff. But, the PR director is still in there pitching. The more problems you have, the more you need a good public relations staff."

Fletcher also had some words to say about "flaps"

involving the Port. "When such (unpleasant) stories are printed, you first have to check their accuracy. If the writer was off base, you try to correct it—without ruffling any more feathers. If it's a case of making a mountain out of a molehill, maybe for the sake of livening up a dead newspaper, we ignore it, rather than add fuel to the fire by attempting to state our case."

I'd underline those first two sentences about "flaps" in dark ink and use a faint pencil mark to underline the third sentence. It all depends on how big a mountain the news media is making out of that molehill. I'm not suggesting that anyone get into a spitting match with a newspaper—when freedom of the press is guaranteed, no matter how big you are as a company, labor union, or even a government, there's absolutely no way you can win. On the other hand, there's no reason why anyone should lie down and be walked over. Just make sure your facts are right and your case-plea is sincere.

Let's now get to the nitty-gritty of news releases, news conferences, and coming face-to-face with the "enemy."

Notice that I said *news* release, *news* conference, and not *press* release or *press* conference. There's a reason for this caution in semantics. In the movie, "The Pink Panther Strikes Again," Inspector Clouseau, played by Peter Sellers, entered a hotel lobby and stooped down to pet a dog. Before reaching out, however, he turned to the desk clerk and asked, "Does your dog bite?" The clerk replied, "No." Clouseau then reached for the dog and was bitten. In shock, he looked at the clerk and exclaimed, "I thought you said your dog didn't bite." To which the clerk answered, "That's not my dog." Clouseau was careless about his semantics.

In the news business, a lot of radio and television

reporters refer to themselves as broadcast journalists and think of newspapers as the press. This difference is a fine line which most members of the news business, print or broadcast, couldn't care less about. But, by using the term, news, you've covered everyone and no one is offended. So why take the chance of raising even a subliminal thorn with some broadcaster by sending him a "press" release, or by calling a "press" conference? Besides, you shouldn't call a conference of reporters unless you have some news—that makes it a news conference.

Late in 1976, a few days before holding a two-hour-long seminar on this subject for some businessmen, I was going through a batch of releases at a monthly newspaper I edit for a labor council client of mine. Out of curiosity, I grabbed a handful before throwing them in the wastebasket and looked at the headings on them. Out of about a dozen, all but one was headed News Release. The remaining one said "Press Release." The really interesting thing that caught my eye was that *all* of the ones marked "News Release" came from governmental or "advocate" type offices, such as a Congressman, HEW, the Sierra Club, and so forth. The *only* one marked Press Release came from a *business*. The reason these businessmen were paying me to talk to them in the first place was because they were having a tough time with the news media.

So much for semantics.

When and how does one use news releases?

First of all, use them as often as possible, which should be about once a month, under normal circumstances. The important thing to remember, however, is that you send them out when something happens concerning your company, whether it's good *or* bad. The worst thing you can do is to keep sending out glowing reports to the news media, and then, when there is a problem in the company, try to hide it, lie about it, or gloss it over. It won't work for long.

What can you do in a sticky situation? Here's an example: Suppose the company treasurer, Sam Jones, is going to be canned for incompetency or sticking his hand in the till. If possible, try to line someone up to fill his job before letting him know that he's on the way out. Then, go to him and request that he resign. If he agrees, everything is easy. A news release is sent out, saying, in the headline, "JOE SMITH NAMED AS NEW ABC COMPANY TREASURER." The body of the news release would read something like this: "The ABC Co. today named Joe Smith as its new treasurer to replace Sam Jones, who has resigned from the position effective November 1. Smith etc. . . ." and then you go into Smith's background and a few items on the company itself. If Jones has been cooperative and has some sort of prospect lined up, you can add at the end of the news release that Jones is planning to return to the XYZ Co. or whatever else he plans on doing, short of cutting his throat.

What happens if Jones doesn't cooperate by resigning and you have to boot him out the door? Simple: you follow the same procedure with the news release—same headline, same body, except Jones' name isn't mentioned until the very end where it's written, "Smith is replacing Sam Jones as company treasurer." Period.

What's been accomplished by this? First of all, you've given the news media a good business story— or even a hard news story, depending on the size and influence of the company or the size of the town. Secondly, if Jones has been a jerk or a crook, you have defused the impact of his activities after he has left the company. There's no way to stop him from talking to his family or circle of friends, but if he starts bad-mouthing you to the news media, the very least you have done is given them a contact name and a phone number on the news release. The chances are much more likely that the reporters will get in touch with the *right* person at the company to set the record straight before it becomes too twisted to untie the knots. The example of the incompetent or crooked employee is probably a situation that most businesses seldom encounter.

The same principle of acting first can be used in almost any kind of situation. For instance, in the food processing industry, food faddists knocking additives to processed food, labor, or higher prices, are usually the problems encountered when the news media come into the picture. Instead of waiting for the reaction to a boost in food prices, and then reacting to the reaction, take the initiative. Suppose you are a corn processor and you know the price of corn is going to go up a penny a can, you could send out a news release saying something like this: "The Corny Processing Co. continues to lead in the fight against inflation. Noting that the consumer price index has gone up 5 percent for the first 6 months of this year, canned corn prices, which are now a penny a can more than they were last year, have risen only one-half of one percent, which is 9 percent less than the rising cost of living, etc."

My figures are probably cockeyed, but here's the point. A grizzled news editor will take that news release and rewrite it. And the first thing he's going to write is that the price of canned corn is going up. But, if he's honest and fair—and a vast majority of news people are—somewhere in that story of his he's going to point out the comparison between the higher rising cost of living and the lower rising cost of corn, and you should end up with a balanced, truthful story. If any company wants more than a truthful, balanced story, it should forget about public relations and start thinking about finding a press agent. The main thing to remember about news releases is that they should be used frequently in spite of the fact that you'll seldom see them in print or on the tube. The news people will at least know you are there and know whom to contact when something does come up. Remember that frequently can mean once a month or once every other month—whenever there is something to say about your company, government agency, or union.

Like learning English in the old days, handling news releases cannot be 100 percent generalized. It's like the "i comes before e" concept. So it is with a news release. The preceding is a general guide to follow. You might also consider these suggestions. Small newspapers in the suburbs will occasionally hold a free seminar on how to get your news story published—in *their* paper. These seminars are usually aimed at attracting the local PTA, Little League publicity chairman, and the Ladies Garden Club, and they serve several purposes for the newspaper. First of all, it gives the newspaper a chance to do a little PR-ing themselves; and second, their editors and writers are probably tired of rewriting eight single-spaced pages about Mrs. Koffee's tea party, or wasting time trying to get more pertinent information about last night's PTA donnybrook, and want to receive that information in better form. The newspaper also has its own unique needs, such as deadlines. Not incidentally, they're trying to be helpful to those seeking publicity. Don't ignore these seminars if you hear of them.

Another very important suggestion you might want to consider is the fact sheet. The news media can be much more competitive than the average business in the free enterprise system. The morning paper in a city will probably run the same stories as the afternoon paper. But, God forbid that it's written the same way. Consequently, if the rewrite man on the morning paper notices that the afternoon paper is running news releases written as they are sent out, he's going to have to write his own story on the subject. Rather than wading through the story of a news release, he might find it easier to work from a fact sheet. Why not attach one to each news release and make the morning paper rewrite man's job a little easier and make him a little happier with you?

## Writing the News Release

Earlier, I mentioned that some big companies and government agencies have PR people who write news releases in a style deserving at least inscription on stone, if not bronze, and yet they still end up in the wastebasket. Obviously, editors are more interested in what the news release says rather than how it's said. The editors are more than likely going to say it their own way, anyway. Nevertheless, there are a few guidelines that should be followed in writing news releases. First of all, make sure there is a contact name, phone number, and address, either at the top or bottom of the news release, and the date for release. (See Fig. 6)

The contact name at the top should be of a person who can answer questions about the news release and its subject. As for the content of the news release, it should either be a fact sheet or a fact sheet put into prose. That doesn't mean the prose of Henry James or Thomas Wolfe. On the contrary, the best day-to-day news writing is plain, simple English put in a clear and concise way. As a long-time broadcast writer, I believe in very tight writing—like *War and Peace* put into ten pages without missing anything important. For that reason, I can't believe that it takes more than one page to write any news release on any subject. Newspaper editors might disagree with that presumption, but I suspect that in most cases they would rather get the stuff in one page rather than two or three if for no other reason than space will be saved in

FOR MORE INFORMATION CONTACT:
John Doe, V.P. PR Dept.
ABC Company
222 Second Ave.
New York, NY 10019
(111) 345-6789

FOR IMMEDIATE RELEASE

<u>ABC COMPANY TO SELF-DESTRUCT</u>

New York, N.Y. Jan. 10, 1977.....The ABC Company today announces that it will

self-destruct in two weeks.  Boom-Boom Nitro, president of ABC, said, etc....

**Fig. 6—Sample news release. Note these features: The date of the news release is Jan. 10, and the story says, ". . .announced to-day . . ." For "in-city" delivery of this news release, the trick is to mail it out on Jan. 9 to every news outlet and hand deliver it on Jan. 10 to the wire services and newspapers. Many variations can be played on this theme, and it's up to the imagination and initiative of the firm's PR writer, or whoever handles news releases, to get the best mileage out of reaching the media. But the basics are always the same—contact name, release date, dateline, and pertinent information.**

the wastebasket. Besides, don't forget the suggestion about fact sheets. They can always be attached as page 2 if you feel wordiness is important. Put your contact name, phone number, etc., on the fact sheet also.

Finally, if you can get the name of the right person, it helps to send the news release to that person. This isn't any harder to do than picking up the phone, calling the newspaper and asking. If it's a business release, send it to the business editor; if a labor story, send it to the labor editor; if a sports story, the sports editor, etc. In broadcasting, almost all news releases go to the news director in radio or to the assignment editor in television news.

There are two ways to handle release dates—either "Hold for Release on (date) " or "For Immediate Release." Not too many years ago, many news releases were hand-delivered to broadcast journalists in the afternoon, admonishing them not to release the story until the following day. The only reason for this was to prevent the little radio stations from scooping the big newspapers.

The only time a "hold" should be put on a news release is if it concerns an event that is scheduled to happen at a later date (such as your speech), and the news is sent out early to give reporters and editors an opportunity to get ready for it. All other news releases should be marked for immediate release.

## Your Speech and the News Media

As mentioned a time or two, a majority of speech consultants and professors consider a speech read to an audience as one step short of committing genocide. I remember reading one critique of scripts called, "How to Give a Dull Speech." The author listed various ways he believed an audience could be bored to death by a speaker, and he made his points through the use of satire. He suggested using scripts or "better yet, hand out copies of the speech and let the audience read along with you." Please don't do that. On the other hand, if members of the news media are part of the audience and you *don't* have copies of the speech to give them ahead of time to read along with you, a great opportunity will probably be lost.

Journalists, particularly TV people, will appreciate looking over your words ahead of time and for a good reason. If a speech is 15 to 20 minutes long, or longer, there are very few TV news crews willing or able to film the whole thing. They have to film minute- or two-minute-long segments of the speech sporadically, trying to guess when the speaker is about to say something significant. With a script in hand, however, the reporter has a chance to look over the speech ahead of time, mark off the important paragraphs and then tap his cameraman on the shoulder when the places to be filmed are reached by the speaker. It not only makes it easier for the TV crew at the scene of the talk, but saves a lot of headaches and editing time when they return to the station—which is good PR on your part. Ad-lib the speech if you like, but if the reporters don't have a script and they have to listen and write at the same time, the chances of being misquoted go up astronomically.

If the news media don't show up for your speech and you think it might warrant news coverage, handle it much as you would any other news release. One important difference, however, is that you should attach the entire speech to the release. Just as none of us appreciate our words being taken out of context, neither does an editor want to see only those words of a speech which you think are important. They prefer to make their own judgment based on the whole, and this can only be done with the entire speech in hand. This can also benefit the speaker. For example, the Republican Attorney General for a western state went before a large Rotary Club during the Watergate era and gave a speech demanding the resignation of

President Nixon. This would have made news had the AG merely held a news conference and read a short statement or if he had just ad-libbed his speech. But he didn't. He read it and the news media had copies of it. The result was fantastic news coverage *including* the entire text of his speech printed in the editorial sections of the newspaper. No chance of a misquote there. But that's not the end of the story. A few days later a county chairman of the Republican Party gave a speech before another audience in reply to the AG's demands and arguments. The entire news corps showed up to cover this event. The chairman, an extremely attractive, articulate, and intelligent person and speaker, ad-libbed his speech. It wasn't bad. There was just one problem—the reporters had to listen and take notes at the same time. The TV reporters would tap their cameramen to record brilliant phrases, but by the time the mechanics of tapping and rolling the film took place, the brilliant phrase had already made the transition into the mundane. As a result, the news space was considerably less, and some of the best arguments were lost. Had the chairman given the news people scripts ahead of time, the reporters would have still picked out the parts they wanted to use, and the end result might have been very much the same as the first coverage. But there was no way of knowing, as there was no script. Also, this particular subject was pretty much of a lost cause. In most cases, however, the battle lines are not so indelibly drawn, and an even break with the press requires some effort on the part of the speaker.

A news release to go with a speech should be handled in the following way:

First, get your news release into the hands of the news media at least several hours before the speech is given. If you want some prepublicity, get it out several days ahead of the speech and put a "Hold For Release Until—" on it. The hold time would be until after the speech was given. In the news release you would stress your main points and quote sentences and paragraphs which emphasized those points. For example:

John Smith, President of the ABC Company, today called for a better understanding of the problems facing his industry. In a speech before the downtown Kiwanis Club, Smith said, "Without the cooperation of the public and local government, we will be forced into massive layoffs." Smith went on to say, etc.

A lazy editor might accept the words of the news release, and let you get by with your favorite arguments. But it is more likely that, without the entire speech, he'll get the other side of the story from your adversaries. With the entire speech attached containing some of the weaker arguments of adversaries, the editor might use those arguments to balance his story without making an exhaustive effort to round up the other side.

In most cases, a speech is only received by those present at the time it is given. But, sooner or later, most good speeches end up, in part or in whole, printed in some newspaper. One of the best recent examples I can cite is the story of a student of mine in the Pacific Northwest Bell Speakers Bureau. After completing the course, he returned to his small eastern Washington community and gave a speech on a subject very vital to the telephone industry—a speech calling for Congressional action regarding competition developing against the established phone companies. His speech was heard by 21 people. But, as he pointed out in a letter back to the home office in Seattle, the local newspaper—with a circulation of 6,000—printed almost the whole speech. And the newspaper, according to the speaker, doesn't even like the phone company. That's what I call mileage from giving a speech.

## News Conferences

There's a group of reporters called the White House Press Corps, which has one special purpose in life—covering stories about the President of the United States. It's not too often the President holds a news conference, and nobody shows up.

State governors and the mayors of cities are also in an enviable position. They normally can send out a notice saying, "The Mayor will hold a news conference tomorrow morning at 10 o'clock in his office," and that's usually enough to assure a good turnout of the news media. Surprisingly, Senators and Congressmen don't seem to have that kind of influence with the news media. Reporters will generally cover their news conferences, but in announcing that they are going to hold one, they usually have to add a topic to their announcement. For almost everybody else, holding a news conference requires a little bit more than the desire to see your face on the tube, hear your voice on the radio, or see your name in print. There's a good chance that you can bluff the news media into coming to a "nothing" news conference, and it might impress some friends in attendance. But, not much will come from it, and it will be almost impossible to get the media back to another news conference you hold. So, the first and cardinal rule for holding a news conference is to be absolutely sure that you have some news that's worthwhile to the news media.

Secondly, the only time you should call a news conference is when you want to cover a combination of areas:

- When you want to reach all of the news media at the exact same time.

- When you want to give them an opportunity to ask questions as a group, instead of at different times and individually.
- When you want to be more assured of radio and TV coverage.

Let's take a look at these three points and see how they work together almost solely by way of a news conference instead of via a news release.

A news release will not reach every radio, TV, and newspaper outlet at the same time, even if the mail service was good. When the release does arrive at the editor's desk and he has some questions concerning it, he has to call you. That means each reporter or editor from each station, newspaper, and wire service must call you one after the other. Calls have to be returned, phone numbers and names have to be written down, deadlines come up, and time is wasted. Keep in mind that if it is a significant story there will be questions to be asked. Furthermore, even a significant story doesn't always appear to be so in the eyes of many reporters, particularly to some of those in broadcasting. Television people especially are looking for "visuals," not words to put on the air. But, if it's a good story, they'll cover the "talking heads" of news conferences and then go out and look for some "B" roll movie film to go with the story.

Finally, a news conference is a lure to radio and television people because, unlike a newspaper, they need more than words to interest people in their news. A television anchorman talking for 30 minutes without any other voices or pictures appearing on the screen would soon find that he was talking to a very small audience. Even his wife and mother would probably get bored with it before long. As a result, almost every news story lends itself to a news conference or interview and assures the viewer that he is not only seeing and hearing the news, but seeing and hearing the people "who make the news." In radio, they use the voices and call them "actualities."

David Brinkley said, "News is what I say it is." Locally, news is what an editor says it is. If reporters from a dozen or more different radio, TV, and newspaper outlets show up at a news conference and walk away mumbling about what a lousy story it turned out to be, they'll more than likely use it anyway because they don't want to be the only station in town *not* using it. Besides, most of them might not be sure if the story is important or not, and so they'll follow that old sheep syndrome. That's unkind. They may just be unsure because of cynicism and might feel that they're the only one who thinks it's not important, and so the story will be used.

Before getting into the actual mechanics of setting up a news conference, let's take just a moment to see who should hold a news conference. The answer is— anybody, anywhere. The owner of a small factory in a small town with one small newspaper and one small radio station (or none) may feel silly calling a news conference to inform one editor or one reporter about an event concerning his plant. But, if it's a big enough story, the news people will come from other towns in the area. If it's a real big story, they'll come from the cities. Bear in mind, even in a small town, the news about a plant closing, for example, could vitally affect many citizens and workers in a wide area.

What's a big story? You'll know before the news people do, or you'll know as soon as the reporters start calling you about a fatal accident, an ecological problem, or labor strife at your plant. In any case, before setting up and going into a news conference, there are certain steps that must be followed, and others that will be wise to follow for the benefit of the news people which will in turn benefit you.

The first step is to pick a time and place as con-venient as possible for the *news people*. That usually means between 9 a.m. and 1 p.m. The morning time will irritate the morning newspapers, and the after-noon time will irritate the afternoon papers because they'll find it difficult or impossible to make deadlines ahead of the other guy. There's not much that can be done about this. But remember, the news conference is primarily aimed at the broadcast media, and the time element is mainly aimed at benefiting the TV people. Radio news is on the air every hour. TV news needs several hours to develop routine stories. Television, like radio, can go live and be immediate, if necessary, on the really major stories, but there are few news con-ferences that warrant the trouble and expense of live TV coverage. Generally then, the best time for a news conference is between those 9 and 1 o'clock hours. I'd zero in on 10 a.m. as the best possible time, except a lot of people have learned this, and so many news con-ferences are called at that time every day that there aren't enough reporters around to cover them all.

As for the place, again it's important to keep the convenience of the reporters in mind. The best place to hold a news conference is a location that is centrally located for most of the reporters, and a spot where parking is reasonably available. In some instances, you might have to travel to a larger city. For example, the owner of a small plant in a small town who wants to announce his plant is going to be closed or that a large expansion program is under way, would be doing the right thing by traveling to the nearest major city and renting a hotel room for the news conference. Be sure, however, to leave all the information with your local news people just before leaving town—and/or even invite them to come along with you, at your expense.

The next step, after picking a time and place, is to

notify the wire services, Associated Press and United Press International. Tell them who you are, what the news conference is going to be about, and the time and place. Then ask them if they'll put it on their "advisory." The wire services are usually happy to do this as a service to their clients, who are the newspapers, radio, and TV stations.

Following this move, send a note to every news outlet in the area where you are seeking coverage. If there's not enough time for mailing, do it by phone. On the morning of the news conference, follow up the previous announcements with a phone call to the major news media—the daily newspapers, TV stations, and a couple of radio stations which have street reporters. These are usually your larger stations.

Having done all this, we again invoke higher powers by crossing our fingers (or whatever method we've established for this invocation) and hope that someone shows up at the news conference. Just in case the media deign to grace this effort with their presence, some other preparations must be made. Coffee and doughnuts should be available at the site. Many of the reporters can't afford breakfast, and it's not good for their disposition if they have to sit around for an hour covering a news conference with an empty stomach.

You should also have ready and available copies of a prepared opening statement consisting of no more than three-fourths of an 8½ x 11 page of triple-spaced copy. The coffee, doughnuts, and opening statement should all be handed out as the news people arrive. By the way, as the person speaking at the news conference, you should be out of sight, while a friend or assistant is taking care of these chores. When the designated time arrives, walk into the room, go directly to where the microphones have been set up, and smile. Look to see if everybody appears to be ready and then ask, "Are you ready?" If not, wait a few moments by pretending to say something to your aide or by shuffling your papers.

When everyone is set, announce that you have a brief opening statement* to make and at the conclusion of your statement you will be happy to answer questions.

After reading the statement, ask "Are there any questions?" If, by some miracle, the newsmen are shy and have no immediate questions, you can make some points by asking and answering your own: "One of the problems/benefits this situation presents is . . . ." State the problem or benefit briefly and give the solution. When the questions from the reporters begin to lag or become monopolized by one person, or if some of the TV and radio people begin to unplug their mikes, simply say, "I want to thank all of you for coming, and if any of you have further questions, I'll be available for a short time. Thank you again." End of news conference. Finally, starting with the decision to hold a news conference, and right up until you begin your opening statement, arm yourself with all the facts and information you can gather on the subject. You may need it.

## The Interview

Whether you send out a news release, hold a news conference, or agree to a one-on-one interview with a specific reporter, there are a couple of things you should try to do and others you should try *not* to do in dealing with the news media. The very first, funda-

*The brief opening statement should never be longer than 40 or 50 seconds. Its purpose is mainly to assist radio and TV crews get started with their filming and recording. It benefits them in a number of ways, including the luxury of editing on the spot by having your script in hand, which means you should follow the script or you'll throw them off.

mental rule is never to volunteer information "off the record" or answer a question asked off the record unless you are prepared and willing to see that answer or information show up later as a quote in the news media. There is no such thing as off the record.

I remember being a hostile reporter during a media seminar at a convention not too long ago and the person being interviewed was set up. I no sooner asked my first question when the VTR (Videotape Recording) technicians moved in front of the camera and started to tinker with the mike, saying "Something is wrong, and we'll give you the signal when we're ready." As they fooled around with the camera, I casually opened a conversation with the interviewee. My remarks were very cordial but geared toward drawing out some damaging statements about his industry. While all this friendly conversation was going on, presumably with the equipment off, the VTR and mike were working just fine and recording everything we said. The VTR would then be played back later at a breakfast meeting of the whole convention, and everybody on hand would learn by vivid example that there is no such thing as off the record in the presence of a reporter. As it turned out, the interviewee was a pretty sharp guy and answered all my questions and remarks with guarded politeness. The lesson was still learned, however, even though it was demonstrated with an example of the right way to handle off-the-record situations rather than the wrong way.

RULE NUMBER ONE: Nothing is off the record.

RULE NUMBER TWO: Never forget that reporters asking you questions work for their readers, their viewers, their listeners, their editors, or themselves—but they don't work for you. Don't try to be "bossy."

In answering questions asked by a reporter, most of the suggestions that apply to speech audience questions also apply here: Never lie, never answer with a

"no comment," have your facts ready   don't ramble—
don't engage in verbal combat with a reporter, and so
on.

## Facing the TV Camera

According to surveys, more Americans depend on
television as their source of news and information
than all other sources combined. That's a terrible
accusation to make about the intelligence of the
American people, since most TV newsmen wouldn't
rely on the tube for their source of information. Nevertheless, we all have to live with the fact that television
influences the thinking of a majority of people, and
what that majority thinks, rightly or wrongly, is the
way the politicians react when it comes to writing
legislation, city ordinances, or federal regulations.
Theodore Roosevelt once described a successful politician as a person who "says what everybody is thinking most often and in the loudest voice."

That makes it easy for politicians to use radio and
television but hard for businessmen. The politician
only has to come up with a few short sentences laced
with such phrases as "people's rights," "business is
exploiting the working man," etc., without necessarily
delivering any facts or detailed reasons for following
a certain course. These short sentences loaded with
rhetoric fit nicely into the time frame of a minute story
on the 6 o'clock news. That minute boils down to
roughly 140 words. Can you imagine a businessman
explaining a new project or the closing of a plant in
140 words? It can be done, but not as easily as the
action can be condemned with gusto in that same
amount of time.

Television is a great source of news for finding out
that a plane crashed while landing in fog and 200
people lost their lives. It's not such a great source to
find out why a company has crashed and 200 people

lost their jobs because of the fog of government regulations, red tape, and interference. Television news is like *The Gulag Archipelago* written for *Reader's Digest.*

A lot is left out, and it takes a certain amount of skill to even get the bare facts across in a manner that isn't distorted. The distortion can come not only in the words that are used but in the angle of the camera. Talking to the people through the medium of television, which is where most of the people will hear what you have to say, requires a little more care than through any other medium. In writing the wraparound to your appearance on the screen, the TV newsman can misquote or distort what you say just as simply as the newspaper or radio reporter. But, an additional pitfall is added by the camera. Here are some steps to follow which will help to smooth out some of those pitfalls!

1. Be careful about your appearance—tie straight, coat unrumpled at the collar, hair combed, and whatever else is necessary to look "neat."*

2. Cooperate with the TV crew. In spite of some of the inferences I might have made about news in general, the TV crews are not out to get anyone, and in most cases, will try to help *you* as much as they can.

3. Try to look directly at the camera lens as much as possible.

4. The camera lens is a magnifying glass; sincerity *and* insincerity both become larger than life. Be natural, be yourself. (Assuming you're honest, that is.)

All the other suggestions—knowing your facts, brevity, having take-away material available for the reporters, honesty, and so on apply to radio and news-

*In the days of black and white TV, white shirts looked like dirt gray on the tube and blue shirts were recommended. Modern technology has eliminated that problem and almost anything that looks good in person will look the same on camera. But, soft pastels are recommended, whatever the color.

paper reporters as well as to the TV news people.

## A Final Word About the News Media

If 15 news people show up at a news conference and one of those 15 slants and distorts your words, the reaction from most businessmen, government officials, and labor leaders is that "the press" is biased and slants the news. The fairness of the other 14 reporters at the news conference is usually forgotten. By and large, news people are blessed with the same virtues and faults as the rest of us and in about the same proportion as the rest of us when education, training, and environment are taken into consideration.

My attempt to explain the nature of the news business as a part of this book on speeches is not meant as praise nor as an indictment, but merely as information which, hopefully, will help both sides in the adversary relationship between the news media and the news makers, whether they be labor, business, or government.

# III
## Quotations

## It's All Been
## Said Before

A YOUNG BOY was once asked to write an essay on Socrates. He wrote, "Socrates was a person who went around town giving everybody free advice—so, they poisoned him."

Giving a speech is like going around giving everyone free advice. But, there's no need to run the risk of being poisoned. Almost any philosophical idea or phrase that we can think of has already been said, altered, re-said, quoted, rephrased, and stolen by at least one or scores of historical figures. "Originality is undetected plagiarism." (I don't know who said that, but it certainly didn't come out of my mind.) In any case, if you don't want to be slipped a lethal "mickey" for giving free advice, as happened to poor old Socrates, or if you want to avoid a political *faux pas,* as happened to Barry Goldwater, it's easy enough to find a quote expressing exactly what you want to say, and then attributing it to some great person in history.

For instance, Senator Goldwater might have been spared some heavy criticism had he mentioned the source of his famous line at the 1964 Republican National Convention. As many people recall, Goldwater said, "I would remind you that extremism in the defense of liberty is no vice. And let me also remind you that moderation in the pursuit of justice is no virtue." Unfortunately for Mr. Goldwater, he didn't mention that his speech writer stole the line from Abraham Lincoln.

As I already mentioned, quotations can be effective ways for starting or ending a speech and they add credibility and punch to our thoughts throughout a speech if used properly. But, it's not necessary to always quote somebody. With a few word alterations, some very famous lines can become your own. Let's take, for example, those immortal words of Thomas Jefferson: "The price of liberty is eternal vigilance." Actually, there is some doubt as to whether Jefferson ever uttered that phrase. The original thought goes back 300 years before Christ when the ancient Greek orator Demosthenes took a verbal cut at the bureaucrats of his day. About two thousand years later, in 1790, an Irish statesman named John Curran said, "The conditions upon which God hath given liberty to man is eternal vigilance." Three score and 2 years passed and the quote became, "Eternal vigilance is the price of liberty." So said Wendell Phillips in a speech against slavery. Preacher Henry Ward Beecher also opposed slavery and shouted from the pulpit, "Vigilance is not only the price of liberty, but of success of any sort."

We now move into the 20th Century. I recently heard a politician credit Harry Truman with saying, "Let's look at the record." Actually, it was Presidential candidate Al Smith who said something like that in 1928. But, don't feel sorry about the Happy Warrior being plagiarized twice-removed. He took that old price of liberty quote, wrapped it in some home-spun and came up with, "Eternal vigilance alone is the price you pay for that liberty."

Had enough? We're not through yet. In his State of the Union Address of January 30, 1974, Richard Nixon gave the quote back to Thomas Jefferson by telling the nation, "Thomas Jefferson once observed that, 'the price of liberty is eternal vigilance.'" But, alas, a writer for the Royal Bank of Canada took it away again in the bank's January, 1977, newsletter when he wrote, without quotation marks, "The price of liberty is not only eternal vigilance, but unceasing work."

"O liberty, what things are done in thy name." Thomas Carlyle gets the credit for that one. But he was born in 1795, and Madame Jeanne Roland, who died in 1793, said, "Oh liberty! How many crimes are committed in thy name!"—on her way to the guillotine.

So much for liberty. A few pages back I mentioned the famous Kennedy quote about doing something for your country which his speech writers had stolen from a mediaeval German Kaiser. This kind of plagiarism happens all the time. The point here is, how can we use quotes effectively?

Here are a couple of examples from my own experience.

During the Arab oil embargo in the early 1970's, I was assigned the task of writing a speech for the top man of a big bank to be given to the top men of some big oil companies. The speech was about the economic outlook for the Pacific Rim, and at that time, the outlook was a mixture of prosperity and adversity. Those seemed like a couple of good words to use at the beginning of the speech. I then looked in my trusty quotation book under Adversity and came up with several good quotes and used this one at the beginning: "In a sense, this mixture is the very best of all conditions. As the English philosopher Francis Bacon put it some 300 years ago, 'prosperity is not without many fears and distastes; adversity not without many comforts and hopes.'" The speech then went on to outline the problems (adversities) and the hopes (prosperity). Near the end of the speech, I used another quote in this way to tie the whole thing together. "Earlier I quoted Francis Bacon, who saw some good in adversity—at least he didn't see it as all bad. But the Roman poet Horace was considerably more positive. In his words, 'Adversity has the effect of eliciting talents which in prosperous circumstances would have lain dormant,' etc." My banker-client was optimistic about the economy in those troubled days. By quoting Bacon and Horace, he strengthened his own beliefs which he was expounding to the oil men. It was the simplest thing in the world to come up with the historical support he needed. All I had to do was look under the word, Adversity, in my quotation book. The quotes by Sir Francis and the Roman statesman not only added credence to what the banker was trying to express, but it helped to give a good beginning and ending to his speech and made him look like a pretty smart guy.

That example is how quotes can be used directly. Here's a way you can use quotes indirectly.

A doctor-client of mine had to give a speech to some 500 doctors in New York about continuing medical education. The key word here is "education." I began the speech like this: "According to Will Durant, 'education is a progressive discovery of our ignorance!' That's a harsh description and I would prefer to say that education is a continuing discovery of our capabilities. In medicine, continuing education and discovery are not self-indulgence aimed at furthering man's pleasure, but rather a necessity to ease man's suffering. Continuing medical education is as essential to a doctor's career as keeping abreast with changing statutes is to an attorney." Notice how Durant's tie-in between "education" and "discovery" are carried throughout the opening lines of the speech. I can't swear to this, but I think all that stuff about self-indulgence and easing man's suffering came from another quote I had read somewhere, but I'll be darned if I can find it today. It doesn't matter, because I know that if I did steal it from somebody else, I changed more words in it than Carlyle changed in Madame Roland's "liberty" quote. Meantime, the doctor's speech was published in a medical journal, but apparently they didn't like the part about Durant. Looking back on it, I'm not sure it made much sense, either. So, they started the speech out with the words, "In medicine, continuing education and discovery are not forms of self-indulgence, etc." Not bad, but it all started with a quote from Will Durant.

For the person who must occasionally write, rewrite, or personalize a speech, a quotation book is just about as important as a pencil or typewriter, which is why a selection of quotations are included in this book. The trick is to be able to use them in an effective way. As already alluded to, there are several ways of using quotations. To begin with, you must realize that almost any thought you can come up with has already been thought of by someone else. ("What a good thing Adam had—when he said a good thing, he knew nobody else had said it before." Mark Twain. "Originality is nothing but judicious imitation." Voltaire. And on and on.)

Armed with the knowledge that a good phrase is already in print waiting for you to use it, you can save a lot of time and frustration by thinking of a few key words on the thought in your mind and looking under those words in a quotation book. The next step is to decide whether you want to quote the person who is credited with the thought, or change a few words and make it your own. ("Though old the thought and oft exprest—'tis his at last who says it best." James Lowell.)

I would recommend quoting someone famous if you want to add credibility to your arguments; to avoid the old Socrates "so, they poisoned him" pitfall; or because the quote—which could be a long paragraph by some recent writer or speaker—says exactly what you want to say in words that are just perfect.

I would recommend changing the words of the quote and making it my own if I already had too many quotes in the speech; if I wanted people to think the thought was mine; or if the thought was good but the words weren't right for me.

In an earlier chapter, "How to Get It Down on Paper," I popped up with the example of the banker who had to give a speech, looked in the quotation book under money, and came up with the Maugham quote about money being like a sixth sense, "you can't make use of the other five without it." It only took a couple of minutes to come up with that example for the sample speech. To which some of you may reply, "Yeh, it sure looked like it, it was so bad." Or, "Who are you kidding, it probably took you two hours." Well, the only way to prove that it can be done quickly is to try it yourself. Think of a subject. Pick a couple of words from the subject about which you are thinking—or the subject itself. Now, turn to "Quotations" (page 143) and look under those words or the subject and pick out a quote that fits in nicely with your own thoughts.

Next, put the quote down on paper, either exactly as it is or change some of the words and make it your own. Next put a lead into it and a few words after it. Before you know it, you'll have a whole page of a speech script. Easy, right?

Do you feel like a thief? You shouldn't. It's all been said before! Remember, plagiarism is when you steal from one writer. When you borrow information and words from a lot of them, it's called research.

Do you recall those professional speakers I mentioned earlier who make hundreds of thousands of dollars for giving speeches? I can't say this is true of all of them, but the ones I know use the same speech over and over again—50, 60, 70 times a year. And hardly a word in those speeches is original. First of all, they tell a lot of jokes which they swipe, buy, or hear from other people. Their "serious" message, sandwiched somewhere in between all of those one-liners, is also a conglomeration of thoughts taken from other people and then put into their own words. Without "plagiarism" these people would be out of business, which would be too bad because their purpose is not to come up with great thoughts, but rather to entertain, and during the course of their entertainment, spread some knowledge around. Josh Billings said, "About the most originality that any writer can hope to achieve honestly is to steal with good judgment."

In the 20th century, it would be almost impossible to come up with an original thought (outside of something technological or scientific). It's all been thought before and it's all been said before. Supreme Court Justice Oliver Wendell Holmes put it this way: "Literature is full of coincidences which some love to believe are plagiarisms. There are thoughts always abroad in the air which it takes more wit to avoid than to hit upon."

One of the neat things about using quotations from famous people is that you can always, and easily, find something to support your point of view, no matter which point of view you hold. For example, the news media love to quote Thomas Jefferson's defense of press freedom. Our third President said, "Our liberty depends on the freedom of the press, and that cannot be limited without being lost." The Jefferson quote the press really likes, however, is the one about "given a choice between government without newspapers or newspapers without a government" he would prefer the latter. Well, that sure as heck seems pretty clear about how Thomas Jefferson felt about the press. Except he also had some other words to say about newspapers. The following are all taken from letters written by Jefferson:

"Nothing can now be believed which is seen in a newspaper. Truth itself becomes suspicious by being put into that polluted vehicle.

"The man who never looks into a newspaper is better informed than he who reads them; inasmuch as he who knows nothing is nearer to truth than he whose mind is filled with falsehoods and errors.

"Advertisements contain the only truths to be relied on in a newspaper.

"Perhaps an editor might begin a reformation in some such way as this. Divide his paper into four chapters, heading the first—Truths, the second—Probabilities, the third—Possibilities, and fourth—Lies. the first chapter would be very short."

What d'ya know. For years, I always thought my grandfather was the originator of "You can't believe anything you see in a newspaper."

Jefferson's position on the press—both sides of it—is not unusual. However, the idea is not to have *the* same famous person on both sides of an issue, but rather *a* famous person on *your* side of the issue. For instance, if you want to say something nice about government, you could quote Theodore Roosevelt: "The government is us; we are the government, you and I." Or, if you want to say something bad, try Elbert Hubbard's "Government is a kind of legalized pillage."

A speech without quotes can be palatable, but to add a little spice, support, and intellectual authority to your arguments, at least one or two quotes are needed.

In case you don't have a quote book, the following pages contain enough quotes to keep you going for a couple of years. I think you'll enjoy reading many of them in addition to the usefulness they'll bring to any speech writing or "doctoring" that you need to do.

## Quotations

### Ability, Genius
Consider the postage stamp: its usefulness consists in the ability to stick to one thing till it gets here.

*Josh Billings*

The question "Who ought to be boss?" is like asking "Who ought to be the tenor in the quartet?" Obviously, the man who can sing tenor.

*Henry Ford*

Executive ability is deciding quickly and getting somebody else to do the work.

*John G. Pollard*

Ability is of little account without opportunity.

*Napoleon Bonaparte*

Natural abilities are like natural plants; they need pruning by study.

*Francis Bacon*

Genius is one per cent inspiration and ninety-nine per cent perspiration.

*Thomas A. Edison*

Genius without education is like silver in the mine.

*Benjamin Franklin*

## Accuracy

Accuracy is the twin brother of honesty; inaccuracy, of dishonesty.

*Charles Simmons*

Even a stopped clock is right twice a day.

*Anonymous*

It takes less time to do a thing right than to explain why you did it wrong.

*Henry Wadsworth Longfellow*

Get your facts first, and then you can distort them as much as you please.

*Mark Twain*

## Action

What you do speaks so loud that I cannot hear what you say.

*Ralph Waldo Emerson*

## Adversity, Prosperity

By trying we can easily learn to endure adversity—another man's I mean.

*Mark Twain*

No man is more unhappy than the one who is never in adversity; the greatest affliction of life is never to be afflicted.

*Anonymous*

Adversity makes men, and prosperity makes monsters.

*Victor Hugo*

Prosperity is not without many fears and distastes; adversity not without many comforts and hopes.

*Francis Bacon*

Adversity introduces a man to himself.

*Anonymous*

God brings men into deep waters, not to drown them, but to cleanse them.

*Aughey*

Constant success shows us but one side of the world; adversity brings out the reverse of the picture.

*Colton*

There is no education like adversity.

*Disraeli*

Prosperity is a great teacher; adversity is a greater. Possession pampers the mind; privation trains and strengthens it.

*Hazlitt*

Crises and deadlocks when they occur have at least this advantage, that they force us to think.

*Jawaharlal Nehru*

Prosperity is something the businessmen created for politicians to take credit for.

*Brunswick (Ga.) Pilot*

### Advertising

The business that considers itself immune to the necessity for advertising sooner or later finds itself immune to business.

*Derby Brown*

Doing business without advertising is like winking at a girl in the dark. You know what you are doing, but nobody else does.

*Steuart H. Britt*

### Advice

Advice is like snow; the softer it falls the longer it dwells upon, and the deeper it sinks into the mind.

*Samuel Taylor Coleridge*

Advice is seldom welcome, and those who need it the most, like it the least.

*Lord Chesterfield*

### America

Intellectually I know that America is no better than any other country; emotionally I know she is better than every country.

*Sinclair Lewis*

A citizen of America will cross the ocean to fight for democracy, but won't cross the street to vote in a national election.

*Bill Vaughan*

I would rather see the United States respected than loved by other nations.

*Henry Cabot Lodge*

Wake up, America.

*Augustus P. Gardner*

America lives in the heart of every man everywhere who wishes to find a region where he will be free to work out his destiny as he chooses.

*Woodrow Wilson*

Our country. In her intercourse with foreign nations may she always be in the right; but our country right or wrong!

*Stephen Decatur*

## Anticipation, Anxiety

Nothing is so wretched or foolish as to anticipate misfortunes. What madness is it to be expecting evil before it comes.

*Seneca*

God never built a Christian strong enough to carry today's duties and tomorrow's anxieties piled on top of them.

*Theodore Ledyard Cuyler*

## Appearance

The world is governed more by appearances than by realities, so that it is fully as necessary to seem to know something as to know it.

*Daniel Webster*

You may turn into an archangel, a fool, or a criminal—no one will see it. But when a button is missing—everyone sees that.

*Erich M. Remarque*

There are no greater wretches in the world than many of those whom people in general take to be happy.

*Seneca*

When I see a bird that walks like a duck and swims like a duck and quacks like a duck, I call that bird a duck.

*Richard Cardinal Cushing*

## Atheism

I am an atheist, thank God!

*Anonymous*

I don't believe in God because I don't believe in Mother Goose.

*Clarence Darrow*

Nobody talks so constantly about God as those who insist that there is no God.

*Heywood Broun*

To be an atheist requires an infinitely greater measure of faith than to receive all the great truths which atheism would deny.

*Joseph Addison*

There are no atheists in the foxholes of Bataan.

*Douglas MacArthur*

## Bargain

Sometimes one pays most for the things one gets for nothing.

*Albert Einstein*

Nothing is cheap which is superfluous, for what one does not need, is dear at a penny.

*Plutarch*

There are very honest people who do not think that they have had a bargain unless they have cheated a merchant.

*Anatole France*

## Behavior
Behavior is a mirror in which every one displays his image.

*Goethe*

Be nice to people on your way up because you'll meet them on your way down.

*Wilson Mizner*

When man learns to understand and control his own behavior as well as he is learning to understand and control the behavior of crop plants and domestic animals, he may be justified in believing that he has become civilized.

*E. C. Stakman*

A man never discloses his own character so clearly as when he describes another's.

*Jean Paul Richter*

## Blindness
In the country of the blind the one-eyed man is king.

*Erasmus*

A blind man will not thank you for a looking-glass.

*Thomas Fuller*

There's none so blind as they that won't see.

*Jonathan Swift*

My darkness has been filled with the light of intelligence, and behold, the outer day-lit world was stumbling and groping in social blindness.

*Helen Keller*

Hatred is blind, as well as love.

*Thomas Fuller*

What a blind person needs is not a teacher but another self.

*Helen Keller*

## Brevity, Simplicity
When thought is too weak to be simply expressed, it's clear proof that it should be rejected.

*Luc de Clapiers*

The more you say, the less people remember. The fewer words, the greater the profit.

*Fénelon*

Brevity is the best recommendation of speech, whether in a senator or an orator.

*Cicero*

If you would be pungent, be brief; for it is with words as with sunbeams—the more they are condensed, the deeper they burn.

*Robert Southey*

The fewer the words, the better the prayer.

*Martin Luther*

There's a great power in words, if you don't hitch too many of them together.

*Josh Billings*

It is my ambition to say in ten sentences what others say in a whole book.

*Nietzsche*

## Business, Capitalism

There are two times in a man's life when he should not speculate: when he can't afford it, and when he can.

*Mark Twain*

It is not the crook in modern business that we fear but the honest man who does not know what he is doing.

*Owen D. Young*

A friendship founded on business is better than a business founded on friendship.

*John D. Rockefeller*

Business is like riding a bicycle—either you keep moving or you fall down.

*Anonymous*

The inherent vice of capitalism is the unequal sharing of blessings; the inherent virtue of socialism is the equal sharing of miseries.

*Winston Churchill*

Capitalism and communism stand at opposite poles. Their essential difference is this: The communist, seeing the rich man and his fine home, says: "No man should have so much." The capitalist, seeing the same thing, says: "All men should have as much."

*Phelps Adams*

## Caution

I don't like these cold, precise, perfect people, who, in order not to speak wrong, never speak at all, and in order not to do wrong, never do anything.

*Henry Ward Beecher*

## Change
All change is not growth; all movement is not forward.
*Ellen Glasgow*

Change is an easy panacea. It takes character to stay in one place and be happy there.
*Elizabeth Clarke Dunn*

He that will not apply new remedies must expect new evils.
*Francis Bacon*

The world hates change, yet it is the only thing that has brought progress.
*Charles F. Kettering*

The problem is not whether business will survive in competition with business, but whether any business will survive at all in the face of social change.
*Laurence Joseph McGinley*

Everyone thinks of changing the world, but no one thinks of changing himself.
*Leo Tolstoi*

## Charity
Measure out your charity carefully—too much help can make a good man helpless.
*Gary B. Wright*

## Civilization
Civilization begins with order, grows with liberty, and dies with chaos.
*Will Durant*

All the things now enjoyed by civilization have been created by some man and sold by another man before anybody really enjoyed the benefits of them.
*James G. Daly*

## Committee
If you want to kill an idea in the world today, get a committee working on it.
*Charles F. Kettering*

When it comes to facing up to serious problems, each candidate will pledge to appoint a committee. And what is a committee? A group of the unwilling, picked from the unfit, to do the unnecessary. But it all sounds great in a campaign speech.
*Richard Long Harkness*

To get something done a committee should consist of three men, two of whom are absent.
*Anonymous*

A committee is a group that keeps minutes and loses hours.
*Milton Berle*

A committee is the safest place to pass the buck.

*Gary B. Wright*

A cul-de-sac to which ideas are lured and then quietly strangled.

*John A. Lincoln*

## Common Sense

Common sense is genius in homespun.

*Alfred North Whitehead*

Common sense is very uncommon.

*Horace Greeley*

Common sense is in spite of, not as the result of education.

*Victor Hugo*

## Communism

The theory of Communism may be summed up in one sentence: Abolish all private property.

*Karl Marx*

Communism possesses a language which every people can understand—its elements are hunger, envy, and death.

*Heinrich Heine*

A communist is like a crocodile: when it opens its mouth you cannot tell whether it is trying to smile or preparing to eat you up.

*Winston Churchill*

Communism is the death of the soul. It is the organization of total conformity—in short, of tyranny—and it is committed to making tyranny universal.

*Adlai E. Stevenson*

Communism has nothing to do with love. Communism is an excellent hammer which we use to destroy our enemy.

*Mao Tse-tung*

## Compromise

Better bend than break.

*Scottish Proverb*

Compromise is but the sacrifice of one right or good in the hope of retaining another—too often ending in the loss of both.

*Tryon Edwards*

An appeaser is one who feeds a crocodile—hoping it will eat him last.

*Winston Churchill*

Compromise is never anything but an ignoble truce between the duty of a man and the terror of a coward.

*Reginald Wright Kauffman*

Compromise makes a good umbrella, but a poor roof; it is temporary expedient, often wise in party politics, almost sure to be unwise in statesmanship.

*James Russell Lowell*

It is the weak man who urges compromise—never the strong man.
*Elbert Hubbard*

People talk about the middle of the road as though it were unacceptable. Actually, all human problems, excepting morals, come into the gray areas. Things are not all black and white. There have to be compromises. The middle of the road is all of the usable surface. The extremes, right and left, are in the gutters.

*Dwight D. Eisenhower*

## Courage
The greatest test of courage on earth is to bear defeat without losing heart.

*Robert Green Ingersoll*

One man with courage makes a majority.

*Andrew Jackson*

Courage is resistance to fear, mastery of fear—not absence of fear.

*Mark Twain*

Far better is to dare mighty things, to win glorious triumphs, even though checkered by failure, than to take rank with those poor spirits who neither enjoy much nor suffer much, because they live in the grey twilight that knows not victory nor defeat.

*Theodore Roosevelt*

A timid person is frightened before a danger, a coward during the time, and a courageous person afterwards.

*Jean Paul Richter*

Defeat is not the worst of failures. Not to have tried is the true failure.

*George Edward Woodberry*

Believe you are defeated, believe it long enough, and it is likely to become a fact.

*Norman Vincent Peale*

## Cowardice, Fear
The cowards never started—and the weak died along the way.
*Anonymous*

The man who fears suffering is already suffering from what he fears.

*Michel de Montaigne*

He who fears being conquered is sure of defeat.
*Napoleon Bonaparte*

The only thing we have to fear is fear itself.

*Franklin Delano Roosevelt*

## Crime
We enact many laws that manufacture criminals, and then a few that punish them.

*Allen Tucker*

We don't seem to be able to check crime, so why not legalize it and then tax it out of business.

*Will Rogers*

## Criticism
I never give them hell; I just tell them the truth and they think it is hell.

*Harry S. Truman*

To avoid criticism do nothing, say nothing, be nothing.

*Elbert Hubbard*

Even the lion has to defend himself against flies.

*Anonymous*

Remember that nobody will ever get ahead of you as long as he is kicking you in the seat of the pants.

*Walter Winchell*

## Debt
Debt is the fatal disease of republics, the first thing and the mightiest to undermine governments and corrupt the people.

*Wendell Phillips*

## Deceit
You can fool some of the people all the time, and all of the people some of the time, but you cannot fool all of the people all of the time.

*Abraham Lincoln*

The sure way to be cheated is to think one's self more cunning than others.

*François de La Rochefoucauld*

When a person cannot deceive himself the chances are against his being able to deceive other people.

*Mark Twain*

## Decision
It does not take much strength to do things, but it requires great strength to decide on what to do.

*Elbert Hubbard*

I hate to see things done by halves. If it be right, do it boldly,—
if it be wrong leave it undone.

*Bernard Gilpin*

**Disarmament**

The notion that disarmament can put a stop to war is contradicted by the nearest dogfight.

*George Bernard Shaw*

Today, every inhabitant of this planet must contemplate the day
when it may no longer be habitable. Every man, woman and child
lives under a nuclear sword of Damocles, hanging by the slenderest of threads, capable of being cut at any moment by accident,
miscalculation or madness. The weapons of war must be abolished
before they abolish us.

*John Fitzgerald Kennedy*

There is no more dangerous misconception than this which misconstrues the arms race as the cause rather than a symptom of
the tensions and divisions which threaten nuclear war. If the history of the past fifty years teaches us anything, it is that peace
does not follow disarmament—disarmament follows peace.

*Bernard M. Baruch*

**Dress**

Clothes don't make the man, but clothes have got many a man a
good job.

*Herbert Harold Vreeland*

The well-dressed man is he whose clothes you never notice.

*Somerset Maugham*

Good clothes open all doors.

*Thomas Fuller*

Clothes make the man.

*Latin Proverb*

Keeping your clothes well pressed will keep you from looking
hard pressed.

*Coleman Cox*

Be not too early in the fashion, nor too long out of it; nor at any
time in the extremes of it.

*Johann Kaspar Lavater*

**Economy**

There can be no economy where there is no efficiency.

*Beaconsfield*

Without economy none can be rich, and with it few will be poor.

*Samuel Johnson*

Beware of little expenses; a small leak will sink a great ship.

*Benjamin Franklin*

What this country needs is a good five-cent Nickel.

*Franklin P. Adams*

I place economy among the first and most important virtues, and public debt as the greatest of dangers ... We must make our choice between economy and liberty, or profusion and servitude. If we can prevent the government from wasting the labors of the people under the pretense of caring for them, they will be happy.

*Thomas Jefferson*

## Education, Knowledge

Education is a progressive discovery of our ignorance.

*Will Durant*

I have never let my schooling interfere with my education.

*Mark Twain*

Education makes people easy to lead, but difficult to drive; easy to govern, but impossible to enslave.

*Henry Peter Brougham*

If a man empties his purse into his head, no man can take it away from him. An investment in knowledge always pays the best interest.

*Benjamin Franklin*

Education is a social process . . . Education is growth. . . . Education is, not a preparation for life; education is life itself.

*John Dewey*

You can lead a boy to college, but you cannot make him think.

*Elbert Hubbard*

I am not young enough to know everything.

*James Matthew Barrie*

Knowledge is like money: the more he gets, the more he craves.

*Josh Billings*

All wish to possess knowledge, but few, comparatively speaking, are willing to pay the price.

*Juvenal*

I keep six honest serving-men
  (They taught me all I knew);
Their names are What and Why and When
  And How and Where and Who.

*Rudyard Kipling*

A man learns to skate by staggering about making a fool of himself; indeed he progresses in all things by making a fool of himself.

*George Bernard Shaw*

**Energy**

The world belongs to the energetic.

*Ralph Waldo Emerson*

Remember that the faith that moves mountains always carries a pick.

*Anonymous*

A law of nature rules that energy cannot be destroyed. You change its form from coal to steam, from steam to power in the turbine, but you do not destroy energy. In the same way, another law governs human activity and rules that honest effort cannot be lost, but that some day the proper benefits will be forthcoming.

*Paul Speicher*

**Equality**

Equality is what does not exist among equals.

*E. E. Cummings*

There are many humorous things in the world: among them the white man's notion that he is less savage than other savages.

*Mark Twain*

We hold these truths to be self-evident, that all men are created equal.

*Thomas Jefferson*

Complete equality means universal irresponsibility.

*T. S. Eliot*

The only real equality is in the cemetery.

*German Proverb*

The mass of mankind has not been born with saddles on their backs, nor a favored few booted and spurred, ready to ride them legitimately, by the grace of God.

*Thomas Jefferson*

There is always inequity in life. Some men are killed in war, and some men are wounded, and some men are stationed in the Antarctic and some are stationed in San Francisco. It's very hard in military or personal life to assure complete equality. Life is unfair.

*John Fitzgerald Kennedy*

**Error**

To err is human; to blame it on the other party is politics.

*Bill Vaughan*

To err is human, but when the eraser wears out ahead of the pencil, you're overdoing it.

*Josh Jenkins*

The man who makes no mistakes does not usually make anything.

*Edward Phelps*

## Excuses
He that is good for making excuses is seldom good for anything else.

*Benjamin Franklin*

Apologizing—a very desperate habit—one that is rarely cured. Apology is only egotism wrong side out.

*Oliver Wendell Holmes*

## Failure
Show me a thoroughly satisfied man and I will show you a failure.

*Thomas A. Edison*

The only people who never fail are those who never try.

*Ilka Chase*

Ninety-nine percent of the failures come from people who have the habit of making excuses.

*George Washington Carver*

A man can fail many times, but he isn't a failure until he begins to blame somebody else.

*John Burroughs*

## Freedom
If any nation values anything more than freedom, it will lose its freedom; and the irony of it is that if it is comfort or money that it values more, it will lose that too.

*Somerset Maugham*

You can't hold a man down without staying down with him.

*Booker T. Washington*

The cost of freedom is always high, but Americans have always paid it. And one path we shall never choose, and that is the path of surrender, or submission.

*John Fitzgerald Kennedy*

We are not free; it was not intended we should be. A book of rules is placed in our cradle, and we never get rid of it until we reach our graves. Then we are free, and only then.

*Ed Howe*

I have always been among those who believed that the greatest freedom of speech was the greatest safety, because if a man is a fool the best thing to do is to encourage him to advertise the fact by speaking.

*Woodrow Wilson*

Absolute liberty is absence of restraint; responsibility is restraint; therefore, the ideally free individual is responsible to himself.

*Henry Brooks Adams*

## Government

The best of all governments is that which teaches us to govern ourselves.

*Goethe*

Good government is no substitute for self-government.

*Mahatma Gandhi*

Government is a kind of legalized pillage.

*Elbert Hubbard*

The government is us; we are the government, you and I.

*Theodore Roosevelt*

You can't run a government solely on a business basis . . . Government should be human. It should have a heart.

*Herbert Henry Lehman*

All free governments are managed by the combined wisdom and folly of the people.

*James A. Garfield*

A government is the only known vessel that leaks from the top.

*James Reston*

Just be glad you're not getting all the government you're paying for.

*Will Rogers, Jr.*

## Hope

To the sick, while there is life there is hope.

*Cicero*

Hope for the best, but prepare for the worst.

*English Proverb*

Who dares nothing, need hope for nothing.

*Johann von Schiller*

## Human Nature

Some of us are like wheelbarrows—only useful when pushed, and very easily upset.

*Jack Herbert*

## Hypocrisy

A hypocrite is the kind of politician who would cut down a redwood tree, then mount the stump and make a speech for conservation.

*Adlai E. Stevenson*

Hypocrite: the man who murdered both his parents . . . pleaded for mercy on the grounds that he was an orphan.

*Abraham Lincoln*

## Idea
If you want to get across an idea, wrap it up in a person.

*Ralph Bunche*

Ideas are the root of creation.

*Ernest Dimnet*

There is one thing stronger than all the armies in the world, and that is an idea whose time has come.

*Victor Hugo*

## Idleness
Sloth, like rust, consumes faster than labor wears, while the used key is always bright.

*Benjamin Franklin*

Laziness grows on people; it begins in cobwebs and ends in iron chains.

*Thomas Fowell Buxton*

The way to be nothing is to do nothing.

*Nathaniel Howe*

## Impossibility
The Difficult is that which can be done immediately; the Impossible that which takes a little longer.

*George Santayana*

Impossibility: a word only to be found in the dictionary of fools.

*Napoleon Bonaparte*

Nothing is impossible; there are ways that lead to everything, and if we had sufficient will we should always have sufficient means. It is often merely for an excuse that we say things are impossible.

*François de La Rochefoucauld*

It is difficult to say what is impossible, for the dream of yesterday is the hope of today and the reality of tomorrow.

*Robert H. Goddard*

## Inferiority
No one can make you feel inferior without your consent.

*Eleanor Roosevelt*

## Journalism
Journalists do not live by words alone, although sometimes they have to eat them.

*Adlai Stevenson*

Journalism is unreadable, and literature is unread.

*Oscar Wilde*

Get your facts first, and then you can distort 'em as you please.

*Mark Twain*

A news sense is really a sense of what is important, what is vital, what has color and life—what people are interested in. That's journalism.

*Burton Rascoe*

A journalist is a grumbler, a censurer, a giver of advice, a regent of sovereigns, a tutor of nations. Four hostile newspapers are more to be feared than a thousand bayonets.

*Napoleon Bonaparte*

## Justice
There is no such thing as justice—in or out of court.

*Clarence Darrow*

Justice is a commodity which in a more or less adulterated condition the State sells to the citizen as a reward for his allegiance, taxes and personal service.

*Ambrose Bierce*

Whenever a separation is made between liberty and justice, neither, in my opinion, is safe.

*Edmund Burke*

## Labor
Labor is man's greatest function. He is nothing, he can do nothing, he can achieve nothing, he can fulfill nothing, without working.

*Orville Dewey*

The fruit derived from labor is the sweetest of all pleasures.

*Luc de Clapiers*

There is no real wealth but the labor of man.

*Percy Bysshe Shelley*

## Loyalty
Unless you can find some sort of loyalty, you cannot find unity and peace in your active living.

*Josiah Royce*

My country right or wrong; when right, to keep her right; when wrong, to put her right.

*Carl Schurz*

## Luck
The only sure thing about luck is that it will change.

*Wilson Mizner*

Depend on the rabbit's foot if you will, but remember it didn't work for the rabbit.

*R. E. Shay*

Good luck is a lazy man's estimate of a worker's success.

*Anonymous*

I believe in luck: how else can you explain the success of those you dislike?

*Jean Cocteau*

It will generally be found that men who are constantly lamenting their ill luck are only reaping the consequences of their own neglect, mismanagement, and improvidence, or want of application.

*Samuel Smiles*

### Machine

One machine can do the work of fifty ordinary men. No machine can do the work of one extraordinary man.

*Elbert Hubbard*

To curb the machine and limit art to handicraft is a denial of opportunity.

*Lewis Mumford*

A tool is but the extension of man's hand, and a machine is but a complex tool. He that invents a machine augments the power of man and the well-being of mankind.

*Henry Ward Beecher*

To me, there is something superbly symbolic in the fact that an astronaut, sent up as assistant to a series of computers, found that he worked more accurately and more intelligently than they. Inside the capsule, *man* is still in charge.

*Adlai E. Stevenson*

### Majority, Minority

It never troubles the wolf how many the sheep may be.

*Virgil*

We go by the major vote, and if the majority are insane, the sane must go to the hospital.

*Horace Mann*

Whenever you find that you are on the side of the majority, it is time to reform.

*Mark Twain*

The only tyrannies from which men, women and children are suffering in real life are the tyrannies of minorities.

*Theodore Roosevelt*

The minority of a country is never known to agree, except in its efforts to reduce and oppress the majority.

*James Fenimore Cooper*

The political machine works because it is a united minority acting against a divided majority.

*Will Durant*

**Memory**

Many a man fails to become a thinker only because his memory is too good.

*Nietzsche*

Experience teaches that a strong memory is generally joined to a weak judgment.

*Michel de Montaigne*

Those who cannot remember the past are condemned to repeat it.

*George Santayana*

A man of great memory without learning hath a rock and a spindle and no staff to spin.

*George Herbert*

**Money**

He that is of the opinion money will do everything may well be suspected of doing everything for money.

*Benjamin Franklin*

The safest way to double your money is to fold it over once and put it in your pocket.

*Kin Hubbard*

The use of money is all the advantage there is in having it.

*Benjamin Franklin*

Money is like a sixth sense, and you can't make use of the other five without it.

*Somerset Maugham*

I'm tired of love, I'm still more tired of rhyme, but money gives me pleasure all the time.

*Hilaire Belloc*

Money does all things for reward. Some are pious and honest as long as they thrive upon it, but if the devil himself gives better wages, they soon change their party.

*Seneca*

Another person's secret is like another person's money: you are not as careful with it as you are with your own.

*E. W. Howe*

### Newspaper

Newspapers are the world's mirrors.

*James Ellis*

If words were invented to conceal thought, newspapers are a great improvement of a bad invention.

*Henry David Thoreau*

We live under a government of men and morning newspapers.

*Wendell Phillips*

The man who reads nothing at all is better educated than the man who reads nothing but newspapers.

*Thomas Jefferson*

Were it left to me to decide whether we should have a government without newspapers or newspapers with government, I should not hesitate a moment to prefer the latter.

*Thomas Jefferson*

### Nuclear Warfare

Idealists maintain that all nations should share the atomic bomb. Pessimists maintain that they will.

*Punch*

The hydrogen bomb is history's exclamation point. It ends an age-long sentence of manifest violence.

*Marshall McLuhan*

We develop weapons, not to wage war, but to prevent war. Only in the clear light of this greater truth can we properly examine the lesser matter of the testing of our nuclear weapons.

*Dwight D. Eisenhower*

### Obedience

Wicked men obey from fear; good men, from love.

*Aristotle*

The only safe ruler is he who has learned to obey willingly.

*Thomas à Kempis*

There are two kinds of men who never amount to much: those who cannot do what they are told, and those who can do nothing else.

*Cyrus H. Curtis*

Justice is the insurance we have on our lives, and obedience is the premium we pay for it.

*William Penn*

### Opportunity

A wise man will make more opportunities than he finds.

*Francis Bacon*

You will never "find" time for anything. If you want time you must make it.

*Charles Buxton*

## Order

Neatness counts; disorder multiplies.

*Dolores E. McGuire*

A place for everything, everything in its place.

*Benjamin Franklin*

The art of progress is to preserve order amid change, and to preserve change amid order. Life refuses to be embalmed alive.

*Alfred North Whitehead*

He who has no taste for order, will be often wrong in his judgment, and seldom considerate or conscientious in his actions.

*Johann Kaspar Lavater*

## Originality, Plagiarism

What a good thing Adam had—when he said a good thing, he knew nobody had said it before.

*Mark Twain*

Originality is simply a pair of fresh eyes.

*Thomas Wentworth Higginson*

When you take stuff from one writer, it's plagiarism; but when you take it from many writers, it's research.

*Wilson Mizner*

Plagiarists have, at least, the merit of preservation.

*Benjamin Disraeli*

About the most originality that any writer can hope to achieve honestly is to steal with good judgment.

*Josh Billings*

Originality is undetected plagiarism.

*Anonymous*

Every man is a borrower and a mimic, life is theatrical and literature a quotation.

*Ralph Waldo Emerson*

Though old the thought and oft exprest,
'Tis his at last who says it best.

*James Russell Lowell*

Everything has been thought of before, but the difficulty is to think of it again.

*Goethe*

## Patriotism

Patriotism is easy to understand in America; it means looking out for yourself by looking out for your country.

*Calvin Coolidge*

I only regret that I have but one life to give for my country.

*Nathan Hale*

Ask not what your country can do for you: Ask what you can do for your country.

*John Fitzgerald Kennedy*

Patriotism is the last refuge of a scoundrel.

*Samuel Johnson*

Love of country is like love of woman—he loves her best who seeks to bestow on her the highest good.

*Felix Adler*

A man's country is not a certain area of land, of mountains, rivers, and woods, but it is a principle; and patriotism is loyalty to that principle.

*George William Curtis*

Breathes there the man with soul so dead,
    Who never to himself hath said,
This is my own, my native land!

*Walter Scott*

## Perseverance

The difference between perseverance and obstinacy is, that one often comes from a strong will, and the other from a strong won't.

*Henry Ward Beecher*

Consider the postage stamp, my son. It secures success through its ability to stick to one thing till it gets there.

*Josh Billings*

Big shots are only little shots who keep shooting.

*Christopher Morley*

Perseverance is the most overrated of traits, if it is unaccompanied by talent; beating your head against a wall is more likely to produce a concussion in the head than a hole in the wall.

*Sydney Harris*

No rock so hard but that a little wave may beat admission in a thousand years.

*Alfred, Lord Tennyson*

We make way for the man who boldly pushes past us.

*Christian Nestell Bovee*

There is no failure except in no longer trying. There is no defeat except from within, no really insurmountable barrier save our own inherent weakness of purpose.

*Kin Hubbard*

## Politics

Politics is not a game. It is an earnest business.

*Winston Churchill*

Politics is a profession; a serious, complicated and, in its true sense, a noble one.

*Dwight D. Eisenhower*

Politics is too serious a matter to be left to the politicians.

*Charles de Gaulle*

Politics is the conduct of public affairs for private advantage.

*Ambrose Bierce*

The world of politics is always twenty years behind the world of thought.

*John Jay Chapman*

A politician thinks of the next election; a statesman, of the next generation.

*J. F. Clarke*

Politicians are the same all over. They promise to build a bridge even where there is no river.

*Nikita Khrushchev*

A diplomat is a person who can tell you to go to Hell in such a way that you actually look forward to the trip.

*Anonymous*

Politics has become so expensive that it takes a lot of money even to be defeated.

*Will Rogers*

## Progress

He that is good, will infallibly become better, and he that is bad, will as certainly become worse; for vice, virtue and time are three things that never stand still.

*Charles Caleb Colton*

There is no advancement to him who stands trembling because he cannot see the end from the beginning.

*E. J. Klemme*

Nature does not complete things. She is chaotic. Man must finish, and he does so by making a garden and building a wall.

*Robert Frost*

Nature knows no pause in progress and development, and attaches her curse on all inaction.

*Goethe*

### Property
Private property began the instant somebody had a mind of his own.

*E. E. Cummings*

Property is the fruit of labor; property is desirable; it is a positive good in the world.

*Abraham Lincoln*

Ultimately property rights and personal rights are the same thing.

*Calvin Coolidge*

### Public
The public wishes itself to be managed like a woman; one must say nothing to it except what it likes to hear.

*Goethe*

If there's anything a public servant hates to do it's something for the public.

*Kin Hubbard*

### Publicity
Without publicity there can be no public support, and without public support every nation must decay.

*Benjamin Disraeli*

I don't care what they call me as long as they mention my name.

*George M. Cohan*

Publicity, publicity, PUBLICITY is the greatest moral factor and force in our public life.

*Joseph Pulitzer*

### Punctuality
I could never think well of a man's intellectual or moral character, if he was habitually unfaithful to his appointments.

*Nathaniel Emmons*

Unfaithfulness in the keeping of an appointment is an act of clear dishonesty. You may as well borrow a person's money as his time.

*Horace Mann*

Punctuality is one of the cardinal business virtues: always insist on it in your subordinates.

*Don Marquis*

**Race**

Mere connection with what is known as a superior race will not permanently carry an individual forward unless the individual has worth.

*Booker T. Washington*

The difference of race is one of the reasons why I fear war may always exist; because race implies difference, difference implies superiority, and superiority leads to predominance.

*Benjamin Disraeli*

I have one criticism about the Negro troops who fought under my command in the Korean War. They didn't send me enough of them.

*Douglas MacArthur*

**Rights**

Many a person seems to think it isn't enough for the government to guarantee him the pursuit of happiness. He insists it also run interference for him.

*Anonymous*

Always do right; this will gratify some people and astonish the rest.

*Mark Twain*

No man was ever endowed with a right without being at the same time saddled with a responsibility.

*Gerald W. Johnson*

**Security**

Too many people are thinking of security instead of opportunity. They seem more afraid of life than death.

*James F. Byrnes*

It's an old adage that the way to be safe is never to be secure . . . Each one of us requires the spur of insecurity to force us to do our best.

*Harold W. Dodds*

Security is the priceless product of freedom. Only the strong can be secure, and only in freedom can men produce those material resources which can secure them from want at home and against aggression from abroad.

*B. E. Hutchinson*

Security is mostly a superstition. It does not exist in nature, nor do the children of men as a whole experience it. Avoiding danger is no safer in the long run that outright exposure. Life is either a daring adventure, or nothing.

*Helen Keller*

## Smoking

To cease smoking is the easiest thing I ever did; I ought to know because I've done it a thousand times.

*Mark Twain*

Pipe-smokers spend so much time cleaning, filling and fooling with their pipes, they don't have time to get into mischief.

*Bill Vaughan*

I tried to stop smoking cigarettes by telling myself I just didn't want to smoke, but I didn't believe myself.

*Barbara Kelly*

The best way to stop smoking is to carry wet matches.

*Anonymous*

People who give up smoking usually substitute something for it—like bragging.

*The Better Way*

## Speech

Speak softly, and carry a big stick.

*Theodore Roosevelt*

It usually takes more than three weeks to prepare a good impromptu speech.

*Mark Twain*

Speak clearly, if you speak at all; carve every word before you let it fall.

*Oliver Wendell Holmes*

Half the world is composed of people who have something to say and can't, and the other half who have nothing to say and keep on saying it.

*Robert Frost*

Speech is power: speech is to persuade, to convert, to compel.
*Ralph Waldo Emerson*

Better pointed bullets than pointed speeches.

*Otto von Bismarck*

## Tax

Death and taxes are inevitable.

*Thomas C. Haliburton*

Never before have so many been taken for so much and left with so little.

*Van Panopoulos*

I'm proud to pay taxes in the United States; the only thing is, I could be just as proud for half the money.

*Arthur Godfrey*

The thing generally raised on city land is taxes.
*Charles Dudley Warner*

The income tax has made more liars out of the American people than gold has.
*Will Rogers*

The power to tax involves the power to destroy.
*John Marshall*

What is the difference between a taxidermist and a tax collector? The taxidermist taxes only your skin.
*Mark Twain*

For every benefit you receive a tax is levied.
*Ralph Waldo Emerson*

The tax collector must love poor people—he's creating so many of them.
*Bill Vaughan*

## Truth
Men occasionally stumble over the truth, but most of them pick themselves up and hurry off as if nothing happened.
*Winston Churchill*

The pure and simple truth is rarely pure and never simple.
*Oscar Wilde*

The truth is more important than the facts.
*Frank Lloyd Wright*

Most writers regard truth as their most valuable possession, and therefore are most economical in its use.
*Mark Twain*

Truth is stranger than fiction, but it is because Fiction is obliged to stick to possibilities; Truth isn't.
*Mark Twain*

Ye shall know the truth, and the truth shall make you mad.
*Aldous Huxley*

## Victory
Victory and defeat are each of the same price.
*Thomas Jefferson*

I do not think that winning is the most important thing. I think winning is the only thing.
*Bill Veeck*

## Vigilance
Eternal vigilance is the price of liberty.
*Thomas Jefferson*

He is most free from danger, who, even when safe, is on his guard.

*Publilius Syrus*

There is a significant Latin proverb; to wit: Who will guard the guards?

*Josh Billings*

## Vote

Giving every man a vote has no more made men wise and free than Christianity has made them good.

*H. L. Mencken*

When a fellow tells me he's bipartisan, I know he's going to vote against me.

*Harry S. Truman*

Voting is the least arduous of a citizen's duties. He has the prior and harder duty of making up his mind.

*Ralph Barton Perry*

## War

Soldiers usually win the battles and the generals get the credit for them.

*Napoleon Bonaparte*

The grim fact is that we prepare for war like precocious giants, and for peace like retarded pygmies.

*Lester Bowles Pearson*

War is hell.

*William Tecumseh Sherman*

The next World War will be fought with stones.

*Albert Einstein*

Diplomats are just as essential in starting a war as soldiers are in finishing it.

*Will Rogers*

How good bad music and bad reasons sound when we march against an enemy.

*Nietzsche*

I have never advocated war except as a means of peace.

*Ulysses S. Grant*

It is well that war is so terrible—we shouldn't grow too fond of it.

*Robert E. Lee*

When war is declared, Truth is the first casualty.

*Arthur Ponsonby*

The Civil War is not ended: I question whether any serious civil war ever does end.

*T. S. Eliot*

## Wealth

He does not possess wealth that allows it to possess him.
*Benjamin Franklin*

Without a rich heart wealth is an ugly beggar.
*Ralph Waldo Emerson*

The use of money is all the advantage there is in having money.
*Benjamin Franklin*

Superfluous wealth can buy superfluities only.
*Henry David Thoreau*

## Will

People do not lack strength; they lack will.
*Victor Hugo*

Great souls have wills; feeble ones have only wishes.
*Chinese Proverb*

## Word

Eating words has never given me indigestion.
*Winston Churchill*

The finest words in the world are only vain sounds, if you cannot comprehend them.
*Anatole France*

Without knowing the force of words, it is impossible to know men.
*Confucius*

Words are the coins making up the currency of sentences, and there are always too many small coins.
*Jules Renard*

## Work

The only method by which people can be supported is out of the effort of those who are earning their own way. We must not create a deterrent to hard work.
*Robert A. Taft*

The world is filled with willing people; some willing to work, the rest willing to let them.
*Robert Frost*

Labor disgraces no man, but occasionally men disgrace labor.
*Ulysses S. Grant*

## Worry

The freedom now desired by many is not freedom to do and dare but freedom from care and worry.
*James Truslow Adams*

It is not work that kills men; it is worry. Worry is rust upon the blade.

*Henry Ward Beecher*

Worry is interest paid on trouble before it is due.

*William Ralph Inge*

## Writer

A serious writer is not to be confounded with a solemn writer. A serious writer may be a hawk or a buzzard or even a popinjay, but a solemn writer is always a bloody owl.

*Ernest Hemingway*

Writers seldom write the things they think. They simply write the things they think other folks think they think.

*Elbert Hubbard*

Your manuscript is both good and original, but the part that is good is not original, and the part that is original is not good.

*Samuel Johnson*

The most original authors are not so because they advance what is new, but because they put what they have to say as it it had never been said before.

*Goethe*

## Miscellaneous Humor

Even if you're on the right track, you'll get run over if you just sit there.

*Will Rogers*

Never insult an alligator until after you have crossed the river.

*Cordell Hull*

Automation is a technological process that does all the work while you just sit there. When you were younger, this was called "Mother."

*General Features Corp.*

There comes the time when a nation, as well as its people, must choose between tightening the belt or losing the pants.

*Howard Tamplin*

Get-well cards have become so humorous that if you don't get sick you're missing half the fun.

*Earl Wilson*

Grow angry slowly—there's plenty of time.

*Ralph Waldo Emerson*

Nature does make mistakes: sometimes she puts all the bones in the head and none in the back.

*W. F. Dettle*

If men behaved after marriage as they do during their engagements, there wouldn't be half as many divorces—but there would be twice as many bankruptcies.

*Family Happiness*

The louder he talked of his honor, the faster we counted our spoons.

*Ralph Waldo Emerson*

I have yet to be bored by someone paying me a compliment.

*Otto Van Isch*

Man blames fate for other accidents, but feels personally responsible when he makes a hole in one.

*Horizons*

All of us are experts at practicing virtue at a distance.

*Theodore M. Hesburgh*

A true gentleman is a man who knows how to play the bagpipe—but doesn't.

*The Wall Street Journal*

Most people would rather defend to the death your right to say it than listen to it.

*Robert Brault*

Get someone else to blow your horn and the sound will carry twice as far.

*Will Rogers*

Inflation is when the buck doesn't stop anywhere.

*Orben's Current Comedy*

Conventions are something a lot of people leave behind when they attend one.

*Capsuled Comments*

The cost of living hasn't affected its popularity.

It's a small world—until it comes to driving in from the airport.

*Los Angeles Times*

Old men are fond of giving good advice to console themselves for their inability to give bad examples.

*François de La Rochefoucauld*

There was no respect for youth when I was young, and now that I am old, there is no respect for age—I missed it coming and going.

*J. B. Priestly*

Youth is that period when a young boy knows everything but how to make a living.

*Carey Williams*

In youth we run into difficulties, in old age difficulties run into us.

*Josh Billings*

For a greater variety of quotations, see *Instant Quotation Dictionary* (Career Institute, Mundelein, Illinois, 1969), and *Familiar Quotations* by John Bartlett (Little, Brown and Co., Boston).

# Index

175